Circumscribing the Open Universe

Thomas DeLio

UNIVERSITY
PRESS OF
AMERICA

LANHAM • NEW YORK • LONDON

Copyright © 1984 by

University Press of America,™ Inc.

4720 Boston Way
Lanham, MD 20706

3 Henrietta Street
London WC2E 8LU England

Library of Congress Cataloging in Publication Data

DeLio, Thomas, 1951–
    Circumscribing the open universe.

    Includes index.
    1. Music–United States–20th century–History and
criticism. 2. Chance composition. I. Title.
ML200.5.D44   1984   781.773   83–23329
ISBN 0–8191–3747–2 (alk. paper)
ISBN 0–8191–3748–0 (pbk. : alk. paper))

Graphic Design: Wes York

for my parents

Acknowledgements

The following materials have been reprinted by permission of their respective publishers.

essays:

Thomas DeLio, "Circumscribing the Open Universe", copyright ℗ 1982, *Perspectives of New Music* (Volume 20, Numbers 1 and 2).

_____, "The Morphology of a Global Structure: John Cage's *Variations II*", copyright ℗ 1981, *Perspectives of New Music* (Volume 19, Numbers 1 and 2).

_____, "Toward an Art of Imminence: Morton Feldman's *Durations III, #3*", copyright ℗ 1983, *Interface* (Volume 12, Number 3).

_____, "Structure As Behavior: Christian Wolff's *For 1, 2 or 3 People*", copyright ℗ 1983 *Percussive Notes* (Volume 21, Number 5).

_____, "Structural Pluralism: Robert Ashley's *in memoriam... Esteban Gomez*", copyright ℗ 1981, *The Musical Quarterly* (Volume 67, Number 4).

_____, "The Shape of Sound: Alvin Lucier's *Music for Pure Waves, Bass Drums and Acoustic Pendulums*", copyright ℗ 1983, *Percussive Notes* (Volume 21, Number 4).

musical examples:

Robert Ashley, *in memoriam...Esteban Gomez*, copyright ℗ 1967, Robert Ashley. Reprinted by permission of the composer.

Morton Feldman, *Durations III, #3*, copyright ℗ 1961, C.F. Peters Corporation.

Alvin Lucier, *Music for Pure Waves, Bass Drums and Acoustic Pendulums*, copyright ℗ 1980, Alvin Lucier. Reprinted by permission of the composer.

Christian Wolff, *For 1, 2 or 3 People*, copyright ℗ 1964, C.F. Peters Corporation.

literary excerpts:

Charles Olson, *The Maximus Poems*, copyright ℗ 1960, Charles Olson (Jargon/Corinth Books).

Ezra Pound, *The Cantos of Ezra Pound*, copyright ℗ 1948, Ezra Pound. Reprinted by permission of New Directions Publishing Corporation and Faber and Faber, Ltd.

...that which exists through itself is what is called meaning.

Charles Olson,
Casual Mythology

Table of Contents

INTRODUCTION

> There is not a phase of our experience
> that is meaningless. Not a phrase of our com-
> munication that is meaningless. We do not
> make things meaningful, but in our making work
> toward an awareness of meaning.
>
> Robert Duncan
> "Towards an Open Universe"

In that brilliant novel by Italo Calvino, *Invisible Cities*, Kublai Khan sits enraptured in his palace as the traveler Marco Polo spins tales of the many fabulous cities which he has encountered throughout his explorations of the great Khan's empire; cities which Kublai himself has not seen - thin cities, trading cities, continuous cities, hidden cities. Soon, however, the emperor begins to notice that despite the young Venetian's very different accounts of these places, the cities have all begun to resemble one another "...as if the passage from one to another involved not a journey but a change of elements."[1] Finally, the great Khan interrupts his discourse: "From now on I shall describe the cities and you will tell me if they exist and are as I have conceived them."[2]

Reality is constituted in the way in which one appropriates the things of the world for oneself. Although for many years modern philosophy has accepted this as doctrine, the work of most contemporary artists belies continuing, albeit often tacit, disagreement over its validity. On the one hand, there are those for whom the artwork remains a closed structure; an object representing a world-unto-itself. For such people, the task of art is to impose order from some improbable vantage point safely removed from the actuality of the present. On the other hand, there are those for whom the artwork represents not a fixed and bounded "world" but rather, as poet Robert Creeley once observed, a process wherein the world as it exists is allowed to emerge and enter one's consciousness. The result is a more open structure in which one's experience is firmly rooted in one's presence in the world and thus could never be viewed as "idea" either born apart

1

from experience or capable of retaining any meaningfulness once removed from the context of that experience. As novelist Alain Robbe-Grillet once noted, "the work is not a substitute for an exterior reality, but is its own reality to itself."[3]

For musicians the term "open structure" has curious and rather limiting connotations. It has been associated almost exclusively with various random procedures of composition, the use of which may, in fact, just as readily yield a closed structure as an open one. In its most characteristic manifestation, the open work seems to be one in which perception replaces object. In other words, the focus of the open composition seems to be not so much upon the object of perception but rather upon the process of perception. It is this quality which identifies the work of composers such as Feldman and Wolpe as well as that of poets like Creeley and Duncan as open, while, in contrast, that of Shifrin or Berryman appears closed. A structure is open if it presents no single fixed view of reality but instead reinforces those variable conditions under which each unique consciousness becomes manifest. As D. H. Lawrence envisioned it over sixty years ago, the open work represents an art of "this immediate present"; an art, the essence of which lies in "the sheer appreciation of the instant moment, life surging itself into utterance at its very well-head."[4]

Since the end of the first half of the twentieth century, artists as diverse as John Cage, Charles Olson, Alvin Lucier and Robert Irwin have embraced this notion of openness as a mechanism for shifting the focus of the artwork, thereby placing the image of an emerging consciousness at the center of the aesthetic experience. In their work, form becomes a model of the self as it first encounters the world and, thus, takes on new meaning as a model for the act of becoming.

Central to this ongoing conflict between the traditional notion of form as a closed framework and its more contemporary open manifestation lie two radically different views of content. Within the closed work, "content" represents a type of metaphysical reflection upon the nature of things in which the self emerges as a static entity possessing knowledge of, but always remaining separate from, all other things of the world. This

2

separation itself stems from the illusion that thought - reflected in the notion of art as "object" - can somehow be disengaged from the process of experience, the process wherein both thought and art unfold and apart from which they no longer have meaning.

However, resonating with the thought and writing of such philosophers as Merleau-Ponty, under the teleology of the open work "the perceived thing [becomes] not an ideal unity in the possession of the intellect...[but] rather a totality open to a horizon of an indefinite number of perspectival views which blend with one another according to a given style, which defines the object in question."[5] Thus, within the open work content becomes substantially the same as process as it is engulfed by that perpetual state of imminence which is the essence of each individual's experience of being in the world. Once again, to quote Merleau-Ponty:

> ...[we] cannot conceive the perceiving subject as a consciousness which 'interprets,' 'deciphers,' or 'orders' a sensible matter according to an ideal law which it possesses. Matter is 'pregnant' with its form, which is to say that in the final analysis every perception takes place within a certain horizon and ultimately in the 'world.' *We experience a perception and its horizon 'in action' rather than by 'posing' them or explicitly 'knowing' them.* Finally, the quasi-organic relation of the perceiving subject and the world involves, in principle, the contradiction of imminence and transcendence.[6]

Thus, rather than representing form as an entity ontologically prior to process, the open structure treats process as ontologically prior to form. Traditional notions of "expression" and "drama" become irrelevant as all vestige of priorness is replaced by process. Ultimately, both the work and the world emerge not as circumscribed objects but as circumscribing events as art ceases to be an abstraction which tries to imitate, symbolize or transcend reality and becomes, instead, a natural event which embodies

3

the world in flux. As the noted visual artist Robert Irwin has so eloquently described it:

> To be an artist is not a matter of making paint-
> ings at all. What we are really dealing with is
> the state of our consciousness and the shape of
> our perception.[7]

The five composers discussed in this book all, in one way or another, have addressed this notion of openness and explored its implications. Each is among the most important and influential American composers of his generation and has had a profound impact on contemporary music in the latter half of the twentieth century. Together their work represents the finest expression of the aesthetics of process and indeterminacy outlined above.

For nearly half a century John Cage has been among the leaders of the American avant-garde. His earliest works, dating from the late 1930's through the early '50's, reveal two fundamental influences - serialism and statistics.   His intermingling of these two apparently contradictory languages led to a series of startling and original compositions, the most notable of which are *She Is Asleep* (1943), *Sonatas and Interludes* (1946-48) and the monumental *Concerto for Prepared Piano and Orchestra* (1951). Throughout the '50's and '60's, Cage attempted to supplant the rather deterministic techniques of traditional compositional practice with an array of chance procedures. Beginning with the *Music of Changes* (1951) and continuing through the *Variations* series of the late '50's and '60's, he explored the notion of indeterminacy in an astonishing variety of ways. In the early '70's, while continuing his work with instrumental and tape music, Cage began to devote more of his attention to the creation of extended text pieces. In works such as *62 Mesostics Re Merce Cunningham* (1971), *Mureau* (1970) and *Writing Through Finnegans Wake* (1978), he developed a series of striking and original poetic forms.

4

Morton Feldman was one of several composers closely associated with John Cage throughout the 1950's. During this period, he sought to imbue his music with a quality of plasticity and spontaneity reminiscent of the work of the so-called "action" painters prominent in New York City at that time. Toward this end he developed a graphic musical notation which enabled him to specify the most general aspects of a musical design such as density, register and timbre while leaving more detailed choices of specific tones, rhythms and colors to be determined by the players spontaneously during each performance. The most striking of these works, such as *Straits of Magellan* (1961) and *Out of 'Last Pieces'* (1961) are remarkable in the sense of immediacy which they bring to the experience of sound and time. In subsequent works Feldman tended to specify his own choices of pitch, register and timbre to a greater degree while always maintaining rather neutral, uninflected rhythm and intensity fields. Those works most characteristic of this period are *Durations* (1960-61) and *Between Categories* (1969). In his most recent works he has embraced a greatly expanded temporal format. *Violin and Orchestra* (1979), a single movement structure, reaches a duration of approximately one and a half hours while maintaining the essentially slow, soft character which by now has become the hallmark of Feldman's style.

Christian Wolff has distinguished himself as the creator of a unique concept of indeterminism in which the interactions among performers are given priority over all other compositional parameters. In his first works dating from the early 1950's, he explored the nature of the creative process itself. Working within strict, self-imposed constraints which limited both the number and type of materials to be used, he studied the various decision-making processes involved in traditional compositional practice. In the late '50's he developed a bold and original concept of musical notation which allowed him to control a performer's actions while never specifying the results of those actions. He replaced all traditional notions of form and continuity with a new concept of structure which focused upon action and coordination. Characteristic of this period are works such as *Summer* (1961), *For 1,2 or 3 People* (1964) and *Burdocks* (1971). Since the early '70's he has become more involved with contemporary political issues. In works such as *Accompaniment* (1972) and *Wobbly Music* (1974-75), he has attempted to project the basic principles of a political ideology known as democratic socialism through compatible musical structures.

In contrast, the music of Robert Ashley stems from a lifelong admiration for American jazz. From the late 1950's through the early '60's he transformed various techniques, gleaned from this extensive tradition of spontaneous music-making, into a new concept of musical structure and developed a very personal approach to indeterminacy. In several works of this period, such as the *Piano Sonata* (1959), *in memoriam... Esteban Gomez* (1963) and *The Wolfman* (1964), he isolated those techniques of improvisation which seemed to invoke the spontaneity most characteristic of jazz and used them as catalysts in his search for new means of expression. Since the mid-60's he has been involved almost exclusively with the creation of an exciting series of music/theater pieces. From works such as *Combination Wedding and Funeral* (1964), *Purposeful Lady Slow Afternoon* (1968) through the more recent, massive television opera *Perfect Lives (Private Parts)* (1980) he has accomplished one of the most successful mergers of diverse media in contemporary music.

For nearly two decades Alvin Lucier has been among the vanguard of contemporary American composers having produced some of the most original and exciting electronic music of the 1960's and '70's. Throughout his career he has demonstrated an extraordinary understanding of the diverse physical properties of sound. In addition, his unique approach to composition has challenged many basic attitudes toward the roles of both the composer and the perceiver in, respectively, the creation and appreciation of a work of art. In the first work of his mature style, *Music for Solo Performer* (1965), he became the first composer ever to employ brain waves to generate sound. Since that time he has explored a variety of sonic phenomena: echolocation in *Vespers* (1969) and standing waves in *Still and Moving Lines of Silence in Families of Hyperbolas* (1974). Each composition has revealed new insight into the nature of sound and has made vivid the subtle interactions which take place between the realms of

6

perception and cognition.

Each of the essays presented in this collection constitutes a detailed analysis of one work by each of these five composers. The specific compositions chosen span two decades of creative activity, from the early 1960's through 1980, and represent a diverse sampling of some of the finest music being written in America today. Together these works attest to the extraordinary impact which the concept of open structure has had on contemporary music, an impact which has led to some of the most profound insights into the nature of human discourse that the arts of the twentieth century have engendered.

1. Italo Calvino, *Invisible Cities* (New York: Harcourt, Brace, Jovanovich, 1974), p. 43.

2. *Ibid.,* p. 43.

3. Alain Robbe-Grillet, *Pour un Nouveau Roman* (Paris: Editions Gallimard, 1963), p. 166.

4. D. H. Lawrence, *Selected Literary Criticism* (New York: Viking Press, 1956), p. 86-87.

5. Maurice Merleau-Ponty, *The Primacy of Perception* (Evanston, Illinois: Northwestern University Press, 1964), p. 16.

6. *Ibid.,* pp. 12-13.

7. Robert Irwin, in an interview with Jan Butterfield in "The State of the Real", *Arts Magazine,* (Summer, 1972) p. 48.

The Morphology
of a Global Structure

John Cage
Variations II

JOHN CAGE

John Cage (b. 1912; Los Angeles, California) studied composition privately with Richard Buhlig, Adolf Weiss, Henry Cowell and Arnold Schoenberg. He has taught at various schools and universities throughout the United States including Black Mountain College and the University of Illinois. In addition, he was music director of the Merce Cunningham Dance Company from 1944-1966. His complete works are published by The Henmar Press, a division of C.F. Peters, and are recorded on numerous labels including Columbia, Deutsche Grammophon, Composers Recordings, Inc. and Nonesuch. He currently resides in New York City and lectures extensively throughout the United States and Europe.

It has become increasingly apparent that the evolution of the arts in the twentieth century may, at least in one sense, be understood as a manifold rejection of the notion of singularity in favor of a broader, more comprehensive world view. "Man himself is being forced to re-establish, employ, and enjoy his innate 'comprehensivity'."[1] Whether it be through the development of a musical language which is multi-centered or through a formal scheme which has the potential for multiple realizations, this rejection of singularity has become one of the dominant factors influencing much recent composition. One need only recall the dictum of composer Stefan Wolpe: "The form must be ripped endlessly open."[2]

In light of this history, it is revealing to examine the works of John Cage, one of the seminal figures in this evolution toward greater "comprehensivity" within the world of music. It is important to see Cage's work not simply as an example of composition which employs concepts of chance or randomness within various structuring processes, but rather as a significant attempt to introduce various notions of multiplicity into musical discourse. Cage's work from the 1950's to the present reflects an effort to eschew any compositional impulse which might result in one unique product, and instead focuses on the total range of structures available to an artist given certain general constraints. Cage's extensive intermingling of chance elements with various compositional processes must, therefore, be understood not as a negation of those procedures, but rather as a catalyst to serious inquiry into the nature of those mechanisms through which structures evolve and are perceived.

One work by John Cage, entitled *Variations II*, will be discussed here. This piece, written in 1961, is the second in a series of compositions entitled *Variations*. The score consists of eleven transparent plastic sheets: six, each with a single straight black line; and, five, each with a single black dot. The instructions read as follows:

The sheets are to be superimposed partially or

11

wholly separated on a suitable surface. Drop perpendiculars by means of any rule obtaining readings thereby for 1) frequency, 2) amplitude, 3) timbre, 4) duration, 5) point of occurrence in an established period of time, 6) structure of event (number of sounds making up an aggregate or constellation). A single use of all sheets yields thirty determinations. When, due to 6), more are necessary, change the position of the sheets with respect to one another before making them. Any number of readings may be used to provide a program of any length. If, to determine this number a question arises or if questions arise concerning other matters or details (e.g., is one of the parts of a constellation itself a constellation or aggregate), put the question in such a way that it can be answered by measurement of a dropped perpendicular.[3]

Any realization of this score is the result of a particular configuration fashioned from some superimposition of these sheets. It will be shown that the sonic structure resulting from such a superimposition will invariably be that of some statistical correlation of several distributions of sound elements.

For the sake of clarity, examples will be drawn from a simpler score consisting of fewer components than the original. This score, constructed by the author, will contain only three lines and four dots. Moving immediately to the first example, by superimposing these three lines and four dots, the following configuration might arise:

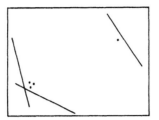

The dots and lines will be labeled, respectively: d_1, d_2, d_3 and d_4; and, 1_1, 1_2 and 1_3.

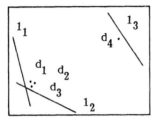

Here the dots represent sonic events and the lines are given assignments as sonic parameters. Let us say, for instance, that 1_1=duration, 1_2=pitch, and 1_3=volume. If a dot falls close to 1_1, it represents a short sound; close to 1_2, a low sound; and close to 1_3, a soft sound; far away from 1_1, a long sound; far way from 1_2, a high sound; and far away from 1_3, a loud sound. Since there is no point of occurrence parameter, in this example it will be assumed that the performer or performers may read through the dots in any order. With respect to this particular configuration, then, it seems clear that there will be three times as many short sounds as long, and three times as many low sounds as high, since three dots fall close to 1_1 and 1_2 and one far away. Also, there will be three times as many loud sounds as there are soft since only one dot is close to 1_3 while three are far away. This information may be summarized in the following two charts:

	close	far
1_1	∴	•
1_2	∴	•
1_3	•	∴

or

	close	far
1_1	3	1
1_2	3	1
1_3	1	3

Thus, the structure of this composition consists of three distributions of dots, one distribution over each line.

It is important to note that two aspects of this structure (this configuration) have been revealed through these charts. First, the total available range of each parameter has been partitioned into two general areas: close (soft, short, low) and far (loud, long, high). Second, a density ratio of 3:1 has been determined. As such, over the course of any reading of this particular realization, one of the two partitioned areas of any parameter will have three times as many sounds as the other.

Next, it should be noted that the configuration also determined a specific correlation among these distributions. Roughly speaking, the majority of sounds will be short, low and loud while only one-third as many will be long, high and soft. More precisely, the 3:1 density ratio is assigned to the two partitions of each parameter in the following manner:

duration:	(short / long)
	3 : 1
pitch:	(low / high)
	3 : 1
volume:	(loud / soft)
	3 : 1

This particular assignment of the 3:1 ratio to the three parameters tends to group, on the one hand, all the short/low/loud sounds together, and, on the other hand, all the long/high/soft ones together. These groupings follow naturally from the respective densities of occurrence within the partitions

14

of the various parameters. In other words, there are three times as many short/low/loud sounds as there are long/high/soft ones:

short/low/loud   :   long/high/soft

3   :   1

Thus, the specific assignments of the density ratio to the three sets of partitions result in a correlation among the elements of those partitions.

To summarize: *first*, the total available range of each parameter is partitioned into two broadly defined regions (low-high, loud-soft, short-long) as a result of the configuration of dots over each line; *second*, an association is made between members of these pairs (short/low/loud, long/high/soft) as a result of the configuration of the lines; and *third*, a density ratio is determined, the result of which will be the sounding of three times as many sounds of the short/low/loud type as there will be of the long/high/soft type. The final aural result is, then, that of a statistical distribution of sounds over several parameters and one specific correlation of those distributions. If several performers were to read through the configuration several times, there would sound approximately three times as many short/low/loud sounds as there would be long/high/soft ones. The order of performance of the dots is irrelevant and will in no way alter this outcome since the overall statistical results will remain unchanged despite the order in which the performers read the dots.

A more precise analysis of another configuration will now be put forth.

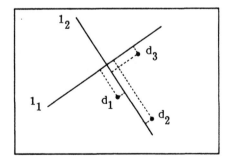

15

Here the components consist of one set of three dots,
$$D = \{d_1, d_2, d_3\} = \{d_i, (1,2,3)\}$$
and one set of two lines,
$$L = \{1_1, 1_2\} = \{1_j, (j=1,2)\}.$$

The first step is to calculate all possible measurements from dots to lines. The number of such measurements is equivalent to the number of elements in the cross product of D and L (DxL). The actual measurement itself may be done with any sort of rule.
$$(DxL) = \{(1_1,d_1), (1_1,d_2), (1_1,d_3), (1_2,d_1), (1_2,d_2), (1_2,d_3)\}$$
$$\text{total} = |(DxL)| = 6 \text{ measurements}$$

The next step is to group all equivalent (=) measurements together. One should note that, as with the first example given above, whenever two or more dots fall sufficiently close to one another they will be considered equivalent measurements. In this example there are three sets of equivalent measurements:
$$\{(1_1,d_3), (1_2,d_1), (1_2,d_2)\} = \text{measurement x}$$
$$\{(1_1,d_1), (1_2,d_3)\} = \text{measurement y}$$
$$\{(1_1,d_2)\} = \text{measurement z}$$
Thus, only three distinct measurements are determined by the configuration.

Given these three measurements the sets of dots can be partitioned by virtue of their distance with respect to each line.

Let

———————————➤ = measurement x

— —— —— — ➤ = measurement y

· · · · · · · · · · · · · ➤ = measurement z

then,

That is, as a result of the distribution of D over 1_1, D is divided into three different subsets: $\{d_1\}$, $\{d_2\}$ and $\{d_3\}$. This partition of D represents the distribution of dots over 1_1 and will be called distribution *.

16

Similarly,

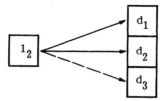

Here D is divided into two different subsets: $\{d_1, d_2\}$ and $\{d_3\}$. This partition of D represents the distribution of dots over 1_2 and will be called distribution **.

The final stage is the correlation of * and **. This will be done with the aid of a matrix into which the two partitions of D just formed – $\{\{d_1\}\{d_2\}\{d_3\}\}$ and $\{\{d_1,d_2\}\{d_3\}\}$ – will themselves be distributed. First, an empty 3x3 matrix is constructed:

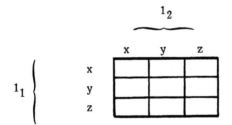

Next, the partition induced by 1_1 is represented by the row sum vector of the matrix, and the partition induced by 1_2 as the column sum vector:

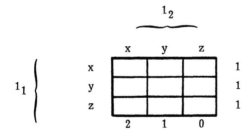

Finally, the matrix is filled in, preserving the values of these row and column sum vectors:

17

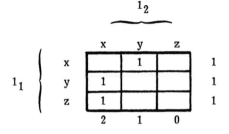

	x	y	z	
x		1		1
y	1			1
z	1			1
	2	1	0	

1_1 (left brace), 1_2 (top brace)

This matrix completely characterizes the structure of the particular configuration under observation. Over the course of any performance of this realization, there will be an equal distribution of sonic events representing measurements x,y and z from 1_1 while, simultaneously, there will be an uneven distribution of sonic events representing the three measurements from 1_2. In the latter case, there are no dots representing distance z from 1_2, while there are two times as many dots representing distance x, as there are distance y from that line.

Finally, there remains only the question of interpretation. Interpretation, in this study, refers to the specific association of L with an actual set of parameters. It need only be noted that differences of interpretation do not in any way affect the statistical structure outlined above. For example, if one calls 1_1 the pitch axis, and 1_2 the volume axis, the matrix shown above can be rewritten as:

pitch

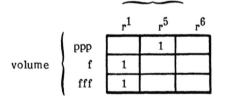

volume	r^1	r^5	r^6
ppp		1	
f	1		
fff	1		

where r^i = register i. Given this interpretation, there will be two times as many pitches in register one as there are in register five.[4] In addition, among these sounds there will be an even distribution of the three dynamic

18

levels. Clearly, whether l_1 and l_2 are labeled volume, timbre, duration, or anything else for that matter, the final statistical result, the structure of the realization, will remain unchanged. So, while each configuration may have multiple interpretations, none of these will ever alter its structure.[5]

To summarize, in the analysis, the dots were first distributed over each line and these distributions were then correlated. This correlation statistically described the final sonic result. Each correlation represents the specific structure of one specific realization of the score; that is, of one specific configuration of lines and dots.

It is, however, important to recognize that the score does not fix any one configuration. Rather, the composer presents the materials by which any such configuration may be fashioned. Thus, the score contains within it the full range of all possible configurations of six lines and five dots and, consequently, the full range of statistical structures to which these configurations give rise. As such, it cannot really be said that any one specific statistical structure is the structure of *Variations II*. Rather, the structure of *Variations II* is the complete range of all such statistical complexes made available by the composer through the score. Indeed, with respect to this notion, it would seem significant that Cage allows the use of many different realizations of the score within any single performance (see instructions: "Any number of readings may be used to provide a program of any length").[6] Thus, each performance may contain many suggestions of the work's inherent multiplicity as it may freely sample from the range of structures which the composition's suprastructure engenders. In order to explore this concept more fully, we must next turn our attention to several aspects of the score not yet considered in this discussion.

In the analysis presented thus far, only the internal structures of two particular configurations were explored. However, the processes involved in actually fashioning those constructs should also be considered, as these too, form an integral part of the composition's formal scheme. With respect to these processes, let us first consider the following information. By dropping any two lines in the manner indicated in the score, the plane R^2 is determined.[7] For example, the following configuration of lines:

19

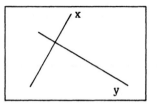

determines the plane:

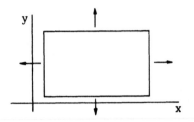

As such, any dots which fall on this configuration may be translated into specific points in R^2.

    Similarly, the configuration:

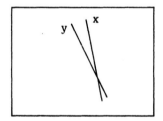

also determines the plane R^2:

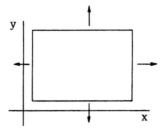

Dropping three lines determines a plane in R^3. However, in this case, the total space of R^3 contains many such planes and each different configuration of three lines will determine a different plane within this space. For example:

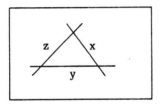

is equivalent to the plane:

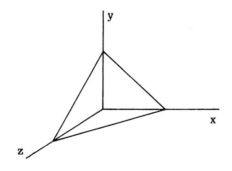

and:

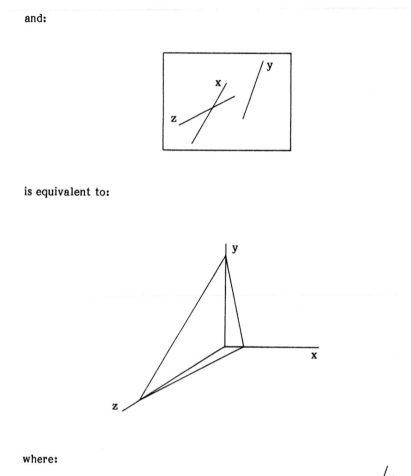

is equivalent to:

where:

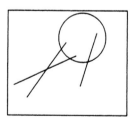

is
expanded
into

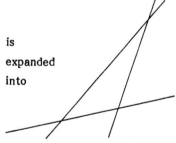

Similarly, any configuration produced by dropping n lines will determine some subspace of R^n. In particular, any configuration produced by dropping six lines, as required by Cage in the instructions for *Variations II*, will determine one specific subspace in R^6. In addition, each different configuration so produced will determine a different subspace.[8] When considered in terms of the creation of sonic materials, it becomes apparent that this act of choosing one such plane is equivalent to isolating one specific range of sounds from among all those available to any given ensemble preparing a performance of the work.

For example, let us assume that the three lines are dropped in such a way as to yield the following configuration:

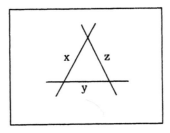

which, as noted earlier, determines the following plane in R^3:

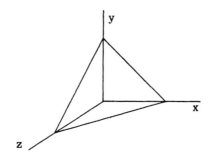

Clearly, any dot dropped on this configuration represents some point in that plane. As such, no dots outside the plane will ever come into the range of the composition. Thus, the dropping of lines determines the field within which all sonic activity relevant to some particular realization will take place. More precisely, it fixes one specific range of sounds from which those to be used in some performance may be chosen.

Next, it should be noted that the act of dropping several dots on this configuration further restricts this range of sounds. First, recall that the dots do not necessarily define specific points on the plane, but may instead define general areas of points. For example, if three dots fell on the configuration presented above in the following manner:

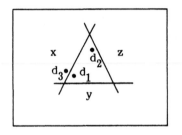

they might be interpreted as designations for the following three areas on the plane:

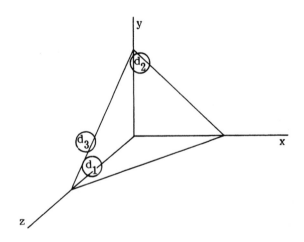

If, for instance, the x axis was associated with the parameter pitch then dot d_2 might represent one specific low pitch (if one were constructing precise measurements) or it might just represent some general area of low pitches any of which might be used as a sonic representation of that dot.

It seems clear, therefore, that one can view the creation of each configuration as a two-fold process. First, from the complete set of all points in R^6 a specific subset is isolated. This is accomplished by dropping the lines and determining one subspace. Then, within this subspace, specific collections are isolated from which the sounds heard during some performance will come. This is accomplished by dropping the dots and so fashioning the statistical structures outlined above.

It is significant that this two-fold constructive process is actually composed into the fabric of the music. Cage has integrated into the design of his piece the very processes through which that design evolves. The structure of his composition, then, is not just one specific statistical distribution which he has chosen, but is an entire range of such distributions and the mechanism for choosing from these. In other words, the work consists not just of the specific characteristics of one specific configuration, but of the full range of all such possible configurations and the mechanism through which one may gain access to each of these. It is a structure the inherent pluralism of which focuses attention on its own generative processes.

The subject of Cage's *Variations II* is not simply the evolution of one specific form from a particular collection of materials; rather, it is the recognition of that infinite multiplicity of structures which any collection of materials might engender. Through his composition, Cage has made available all the possible variants of one type of structure, but has himself singled out none in particular to be the specific form of the work. *Variations II* is, then, one large comprehensive system which represents the total accumulation of its many constituent realizations. Encountering such a global structure, one is reminded of the writings of Buckminster Fuller, a philosopher whose influence John Cage has often acknowledged:[9]

We have now updated our definitions of

the universe by conforming them with the most recent and erudite scientific findings of Einstein and Plank. Earlier in our thinking we discovered man's function in the universe to be that of the most effective metaphysical capability experimentally evidenced thus far within our locally observable phases and time zones of universe. We have also discovered that it is humanity's task to comprehend and set in order the special case facts of human experience and to win therefrom knowledge of the *a priori existence of a complex of generalized abstract principles which apparently altogether govern all physically evolving phenomena of the universe*.[10]

Cage's entire *Variations* series carries on the inquiry into such notions of global structure in a variety of fascinating ways. Through these works, Cage directly confronts one of the central issues addressed by artists throughout the twentieth century and rigorously explores, for his medium, those notions of "comprehensivity" which so much modern thought has come to embrace.

1.   R. Buckminster Fuller, *Operating Manual for Spaceship Earth* (New York: Simon and Schuster, 1969), p. 44.

2.   Stefan Wolpe, "Thinking Twice" in *Contemporary Composers on Contemporary Music*, Barney Childs and Elliott Schwartz, eds. (New York: Holt, Rinehart and Winston, Inc., 1967), p. 302.

3.   John Cage, *Variations II* (New York: Henmar Press Inc., 1961), p.1.

4.   Notation of registers: middle C is labeled C^4, the C one octave higher is C^5 and so forth; the C one octave lower is C^3 and so forth. All tones between C^i and C^j , where i and j are adjacent integers, are given the superscript i and so fall within register i.

5.   It should be noted that, once again for the sake of simplicity, it is assumed that all instruments used in a performance will have approximately the same range of variability over each of the sonic parameters involved. Of course, if this were not the case, each group of instruments within the total ensemble which have approximately the same range would independently sound the constructed distribution and the total result would be several proportionally related reflections of a single distribution.

6.   Cage, *op. cit.*, p. 1.

7.   In this paper, R^2 is the symbol for 2-dimensional space; R^3, the symbol for 3-dimensional space; and R^n, the symbol for n-dimensional space.

8.   Herein lies one difference between *Variations II* and its predecessor *Variations I*. In the earlier work, only five configurations of lines were fixed by the composer and were to be used for every performance. As such, only five subspaces are is ever employed in *Variations I*.

9.   Indeed, in many respects, the structure of *Variations II* is quite similar to those which Fuller calls synergetic systems - systems which are "unpredicated by the separately observed behaviors of any of the system's separate parts or any subassembly of the system's parts." (Fuller, *op. cit.*, p.71.)

10.   Fuller, *op. cit.*, p. 121.

Toward an Art
of Imminence

Morton Feldman
Durations III

MORTON FELDMAN

Morton Feldman (b. 1926; New York, New York) studied composition privately with Wallingford Riegger and Stefan Wolpe. Throughout the 1950's and 60's he was closely associated with various painters of the New York School and wrote extensively on their work for magazines such as *Art in America* and *Arts*. His works are published by C.F. Peters and Universal Editions. Several are recorded on such labels as Composers Recordings, Inc., Columbia Odyssey and Mainstream. He currently is the Edgard Varese Professor of Composition at the State University of New York at Buffalo.

Traditionally, a work of art was conceived as a fixed object, bounded and circumscribed by a finite set of relations born of some personal aesthetic impulse. Since the 1950's, however, dramatic changes in attitudes toward the creative process have called into question this very notion of art and the critical position which supports it. The most progressive composers, artists and writers of this period have come to recognize that the art object is itself nothing more than a remnant of activity. It is the end product of a series of events which constitute its perceptual and conceptual framework; a framework within which the object must constantly resonate if it is to remain in any sense meaningful.

During the 1950's, along with various members of the so-called New York school of painters and Black Mountain poets, Morton Feldman became one of the first to conceive and execute an art completely freed from any vestige of *a priori* compositional rhetoric. As the foundation of his new art, Feldman proposed a language of pure process. In his art, the work and the act of creation became indistinguishable.

Typically, a piece of music evolves through a series of transformations during which raw materials are carefully molded into a particular unique configuration which is then identified as the artwork. Sketches and drafts are constantly replaced or discarded as the composer slowly fashions the particular structure which he desires. Feldman, in contrast, seems to engage the entirety of this process within the very perceptible framework of his compositions. For him, the act of creating a piece becomes the very substance of that piece - its form, in a rich new sense of the word.

Another striking example of this attitude toward art is found in the work of the poet Charles Olson. In Olson's view: "The motive...of reality is process not goal."[1] To this, critic Robert von Hallberg has added several illuminating observations:

> One normally expects a poet to blot out
> his first thoughts after they have led to

subsequent, more precise and refined formula-
tions, in the name of craft and artistry, not to
mention brevity. But these expectations grow
from...an aesthetic theory...[in which] the
artifact is achievement and result. 'Artifact' is
not even an adequate term to use in discussing
[Olson's works]: *they are not the result of
Olson's labors; they are his labors.*[2]

Thus, for example, throughout his Maximus cycle, whenever Olson refines
an idea, he does so within the very context of the poem itself rather than
from some improbable vantage point outside of it or in any sense prior to
it. In one striking instance, as his Maximus persona looks up at a statue of
Our Lady of Good Voyage, which stands on top of a church overlooking
Gloucester harbor, he continually corrects his observations and impressions
until he finally comes to an accurate representation of the scene. The
passage concludes as a clear picture of the object, which the figure is
holding in its arms, bursts forth into consciousness:

(o my lady of good voyage
in whose arm, whose left arm rests
no boy but a carefully carved wood, a painted face,
a schooner!
a delicate mast, as bow-sprit for

forwarding

(*The Maximus Poems I,2*)[3]

To experience art such as this is quite literally to experience the act
of creation "in medias res" and the work in the act of being born. What the
perceiver witnesses is the very emergence of order; the artwork organizing
itself into existence. Thus, as it was for a philosopher such as Merleau-
Ponty, so it seems that for Olson and Feldman:

... the perceived thing is not an ideal unity in
the possession of the intellect...; it is, rather, a
totality open to a horizon of an indefinite
number of perspectival views.[4]

Through their art, perception and creation are revealed as one and
the same act. Each of their works appears to be born at the instant of

one's appropriation of its elements.

Among the works of Morton Feldman, none more clearly and concisely exemplifies this attitude toward composition than his series entitled *Durations*, the third of which consists of four pieces, scored for the unusual combination of violin, tuba and piano. The third piece of this set will be considered here. The score is reprinted on the following page. The instructions read as follows:

> The first sound [is played by] all instru-
> ments simultaneously. The duration of each
> sound is chosen by the performer. All beats are
> slow. All sounds should be played with a
> minimum of attack. Grace notes should not be
> played too quickly. Numbers between sounds
> indicate silent beats. Dynamics are very low.[5]

The work opens in stasis. A single three note sonority is repeated over and over again. There seems to be no functioning linear structure. Rather, the sounds appear to be organized only as a succession of isolated vertical configurations. Gradually, however, this situation begins to change. As the piece proceeds, the initial sonority breaks apart, its constituent elements taking on functions independent of their role within that particular sound. Over the course of this transformation, one instrument, the tuba, emerges as predominant - twice uttering highly organized linear formations, each an extension of the initial three tones of the piece. As these new structures evolve, the violin and piano continue to sound the original cluster which now, however, clearly functions as a backdrop to the lines unfolding in the tuba part. Eventually, the purely vertical format of the opening is transformed into an exclusively linear one and the work concludes with an unaccompanied tuba solo. From the single three note sonority which opened the piece, a complex foreground/background dualism emerges.

For the purposes of analysis, each vertical sonority has been numbered (see score, following page). This procedure has been adopted in spite of the degree of rhythmic freedom involved in any performance for,

Durations

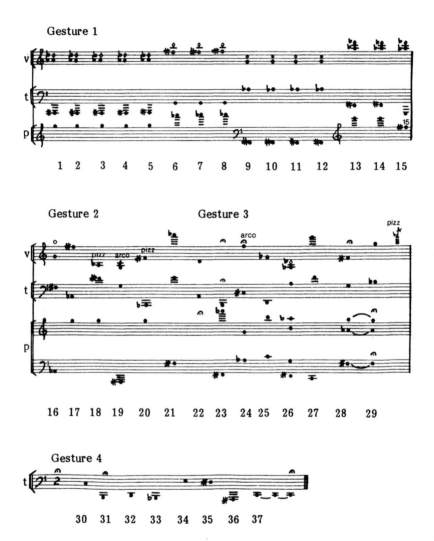

as the composer himself notes, each vertical configuration is to be treated
as a relatively integrated sonic event:

> In the *Durations* with the tuba, the
> weight of the three instruments made me treat
> them as one. I wrote all sounds simultaneously
> knowing that no instrument would ever be too
> far behind or too far ahead of the other.[6]

Also, to help organize the discussion, the piece has been divided into four
segments labeled "gestures." These are (as marked in the score):

> Gesture 1: sonorities 1 - 15
> Gesture 2: sonorities 16 - 21
> Gesture 3: sonorities 22 - 29
> Gesture 4: sonorities 30 - 37

The reasons which support this particular partitioning of the work will
become clear as the analysis proceeds. As it is intended here, the word
"gesture" is roughly analogous to the term "phrase", though in this context,
the former is clearly preferable. "Gesture" has fewer connotations of
closure and Feldman's music is generally far too continuous in its unfoldings
to be properly considered in terms of distinct, separable parts. However, in
order to coordinate discussion of the piece, the use of some term was felt
to be necessary and "gesture" seemed most appropriate.

The first gesture of the composition (sonorities 1-15) consists
entirely of a gradual acceleration of rhythmic activity over a relatively
static pitch and register field. The first distinct sound of the piece is heard
five times in succession (sonorities 1-5); the second, three times (6-8); the
third, four times (9-12); the fourth, two times (13-14); and the fifth, only
once (15). In general, sonorities at the opening of the passage are
prolonged for rather lengthy periods of time and thus seem to change from
one to another at a rather slow pace. Toward the end of the passage,
however, the sounds are not repeated as frequently and therefore, change
far more rapidly.

Despite this acceleration, the passage is, in many other respects,
quite static. First of all, in terms of pitch content, it consists entirely of a

35

single three note cluster - F#, G, A^b. From this basic pitch material, the first fourteen of its fifteen sonorities are fashioned with the aid of the following simple permutation scheme (the fifteenth and final sonority is transitional and will be discussed later):

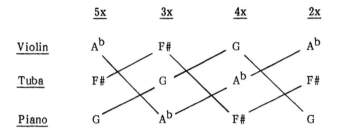

Such a procedure ensures that all three pitches will be present at all times, in equal abundance, and that none will be given undue emphasis.

Secondly, the registral distribution of tones is quite constant. The highest and lowest extremes are always present but, with only one exception, the mid-range (ca. C^3-C^5) remains empty:[7]

In addition, the tuba and violin each tend to be associated with one particular register (a fact undoubtedly due to their specific ranges). The violin invariably sounds in the highest register while the tuba, with one exception, appears in the lowest. Significantly, however, according to theorists Robert Cogan and Pozzi Escot:

> The resonance region of the tuba is

between 100 and 300 cps ca. G^2-D^4 ... thus, in the lower half of the range ca. C^1-$F\#^2$ ...energy lies in the second to fourth partials.[8]

As such, though the tones which are played by the tuba are almost all located in the lowest registers, much of the sonic energy is actually placed in the mid-range foreshadowing the shift to this region, which takes place in Gesture 2. Of course, this change is also prepared by the single fundamental tone sounded by the tuba in its upper register (sonorities 8-12).

Finally, certain pitches tend to be associated with specific registers and, as a result, are quite frequently repeated within the same octave. With one exception, A^b appears only in the upper register while F# generally sounds in the lowest. These factors all play a crucial role in determining the more static side of the passage.

As noted earlier, the final sonority of Gesture 1 must be viewed as transitional. While it does not arise from the proper continuation of the permutation scheme outlined above, it does reflect many other qualities characteristic of the music which precedes it. It maintains the same wide registral spacing and repeats the same high A^b found in the previous two sonorities. Thus, while it continues to prolong the general sonic character of the opening gesture, it also, for the first time, breaks the permutation scheme in preparation for the music which is about to unfold in Gesture 2. Significantly, that scheme does return briefly in sonorities 15, 16 and 17, effecting a smooth transition from Gesture 1 to Gesture 2.

The second gesture of the composition (sonorities 16-21) continues to prolong the same three note cluster which constituted the entire pitch collection of Gesture 1. There are several other factors, however, which clearly distinguish this music from that which preceded it. First of all, the permutation scheme which operated throughout almost all of the first gesture is abandoned. Also, there are no exact repetitions of entire sonorities as there were earlier. As a result, the music of this passage is altogether more active than that which preceded it. Finally, the activity of Gesture 2 incorporates those registers which up until this point were left relatively barren - a development which, as noted earlier, was prepared quite thoroughly in Gesture 1.

16   17   18   19   20   21

This change in spatial disposition is immediately apparent. In the first half of the passage (sonorities 16, 17, and 18) the outer registers are completely abandoned in favor of the central regions (ca. A^{b2}-G^6). By the middle of the passage, however, this situation begins to reverse itself and the music starts to expand back outward to the extremities of Gesture 1. First, the low register returns in sonority 19 with the tone F♯ which predominated in that register through the initial gesture and which, in fact, opened the piece in that octave. Then, in sonority 21, the upper region returns with a sounding of high A^b which predominated in that register throughout Gesture 1 and which also opened the piece in that octave. In addition, throughout most of the second gesture, G is fixed in the very same register in which it appeared in the opening sonority. However, while the composer clearly reflects back to the wide spacing of the initial sounds of the piece, he still maintains some sonic presence in the mid-range, a characteristic, of course, of sonorities 16 through 21. Thus, while the music of Gesture 2 expands into new dimensions, it also reaches back to its origins, assimilating into this new material the very first sound of the piece.

As with register, so too the use of timbre is at least initially quite different from that found in Gesture 1. With respect to the violin, throughout the initial gesture, only harmonics were used. Now, in contrast,

38

the string color shifts constantly, first from harmonics to normal sound and then, finally, to pizzicato. Similarly, throughout Gesture 1, the tuba focused primarily upon its lowest register while, in the second gesture, it expands into the upper limits of its range - a significant development which sets the stage for the distinctly bi-leveled registral structure of the music which will be heard in Gestures 3 and 4. This change in register also highlights certain characteristics of the instrument's tone color. Again, according to Cogan and Escot:

> There is a marked contrast between the
> lower half of the range, where the energy lies in
> the second to fourth partials, and the upper half
> whose tones approximate pure sine tones.[9]

These are precisely the two regions upon which Feldman gradually focuses his attention.

Gesture 2 is also, in many ways, quite static, a fact which helps maintain continuity and effects a smooth transition between the two gestures. First of all, while the spatial disposition of tones is more active and variable, there is a clear tendency for G to appear as the highest sounding tone of the cluster, F# to be in the middle and A^b on the bottom. This is true without exception throughout the first half of the passage and changes only as the registers expand outward, recapturing the sonorities of Gesture 1. In addition, particular tones are quite often fixed within specific registers. The most prominent of these is the tone G which repeats in the same octave five of the six times it sounds over the course of this passage.

Thus, as with Gesture 1, the structure of this second gesture may be summarized as a movement from stasis to activity, expanding both the degree and kind of motion which preceded it. Individual sonorities are never repeated in their entirety. Timbre changes frequently and register becomes quite variable. Throughout, however, there is an ever increasing amount of pitch/register association which helps draw the listener back to the very first sonority of the composition. As a result, despite all the changes which have taken place, the music continues to resonate with the source of its unfoldings.

The third gesture continues this dual process of prolonging the original sonority while expanding ever farther into new sonic dimensions. For the first time new pitches are introduced into the original cluster. The instruments begin to take on new, more independent roles as a result of which the texture starts to fragment – a tendency also promoted by the use of fermatas within the individual parts. In addition, for the first time, the piano introduces simultaneities into the texture and assumes the function which previously had been assigned to all three instruments. It alone continues to prolong the original sonority as a verticality. On the other hand, the tuba part, which now consists almost entirely of new tones, emerges as a purely linear construction. As a result of this dichotomy, the tuba tends to locate itself as foreground while the piano appears to recede into a supporting position as background.

The opening of Gesture 3 is marked by the sounding of new pitches. Over the course of this passage all but two tones of the complete chromatic collection are heard. Specifically, the violin and piano each introduce two new pitches while continuing to prolong the original sonority, with frequent echoes of the pitch disposition of the opening (F# in the lower regions, A^b on top). However, within each of these instrumental parts, the original three note cell remains predominant. The two new pitches introduced by the violin, D and F, each sound only once while the original three tones sound twice each. Similarly, the two new pitches introduced by the piano are each heard two times while, of the original three, F# and G each sound three times and A^b sounds four times.

The tuba part, in contrast, consists primarily of new pitches and, as such, abandons almost all pitch reference to the original sonority. Of the eight tones which the tuba sounds, all but one, G, are new. In addition, the tuba part emerges as the first organized linear configuration of the composition. Its eight tones are evenly divided into two related tetrachords each of which opens with the same pitch, A – the only repeated tone in the line. These tetrachords are divided into two distinct registers which fall quite clearly into the two characteristic tone color regions identified by Cogan and Escot and discussed earlier.

2   2   1   4   2   3

In addition, the total interval content of each of these tetrachords is identical (as is common practice, all intervals are labeled in their smallest form):[10]

1	2	3	4	5	6		- interval
1	2	1	1	1	0		- frequency of appearance within tetrachord

Within the composition, the four tones of the first tetrachord are ordered in such a way that only the intervals 1 and 2 sound:

2   2   1

The ordering of the second hexachord excludes 1 but allows 3 and 4 to sound along with 2:

4   2   3

41

At this time, it is important to recall that the predominant sound of the piece, the trichord (F#, G, A^b) consists entirely of the intervals 1 and 2. Thus, despite the fact that the first tetrachord contains no pitches in common with this sonority, there is a striking intervallic consistency between them, as both project the same two intervals. At least initially, then, the tuba line of Gesture 3 appears as an outgrowth of that trichord which, thus far, has dominated the composition.

The tetrachords heard in this passage afford the opportunity to sound new intervallic material not available under the severe restrictions of the F#, G, A^b trichord. This potential is realized in the second tetrachord where the four tones are ordered in such a way that two new intervals, 3 and 4, are drawn out of the collection. Thus, from the original three note cluster, unfolds an independent, highly structured linear formation which, after first revealing its roots within that sonority, proceeds to expand its sonic boundaries. In response, the original cluster itself takes on new meaning as the source of all that has transpired. Each determines the other's function. As the foreground emerges, so too the background is defined.

It is also interesting to note that the tones of the first tetrachord are themselves spread out over two registers. The first and third notes outline a 4 (A - C$^#$), while the second and fourth outline a 3 (B - D). These prepare the listener for the 3 and 4 of the second tetrachord. Moreover, the specific 3 (B^1 - D^2) outlined in the low register in the first tetrachord of Gesture 3 is made explicit in the very same register in the first tetrachord of Gesture 4, effecting another smooth transition between successive gestures.

The fourth and last gesture of the composition confirms the predominance of those elements just beginning to emerge as foreground in the previous eight sonorities. This passage consists of an unaccompanied solo for tuba which serves to reiterate, as well as extend, the music preceding it. First, it opens with a two note figure which is very similar to the one initiating the tuba line in the third gesture. As if to isolate this similarity, in both cases the figure is separated by a fermata. In addition, this solo also contains eight pitches, only one of which, F#, is found in the original trichord. Finally, the composer introduces the two remaining tones needed to complete the full chromatic collection, D# and E.

As before, with the aid of a single repeated tone and some shifting of registers, these eight pitches also partition into two distinct tetrachords:

1   3   4   1   3   6

In this case, however, the first tetrachord opens with the same tone which concludes the second tetrachord, a variation which adds a feeling of closure not inappropriate to the final gesture of the composition. Moreover, each tetrachord opens in the same register and then descends approximately one octave. Each begins on tones within the instrument's resonance region, the region characterized by the sine tone color, and then descends to lower registers producing richer sonorities. These descending motions seem to reverse, in microcosm, the predominantly ascending movement characteristic of the tuba thus far in the composition. In general, however, the tuba here lies much lower than it did in Gesture 3 and tends to focus upon regions not heard since Gesture 1. This remarkable similarity to the opening helps to draw out latent associations between the linear configuration which concludes the piece and vertical sonority which opened it.

Once again, of greatest importance is the interval content of these two tetrachords. The total interval content of the first is very similar to that of both tetrachords of Gesture 3 in that it continues to emphasize seconds and introduces no new intervals.

1	2	3	4	5	6
2	2	1	1	0	0

That of the second is somewhat different most notably in the addition of a tritone and the emphasis on 3:

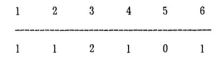

1	2	3	4	5	6
1	1	2	1	0	1

The tritone is the only interval which, up until now, has not been available either from the original trichord, which contained only 1 and 2, or from the two tetrachords of Gesture 3, which contained 1, 2, 3, 4 and 5.

The actual sounding intervals seem to reinforce this sense of expansion. The first tetrachord presents 1, 3 and 4, reiterating the intervallic language which characterized the preceding gesture. Then, the 1, 3 and 6 are sounded. The 1 and 3 provide continuity as they are carried over from the previous four notes. The 6, however, is the last interval to be brought into the world which has evolved from the initial cluster and, significantly, is the last sounding interval of the composition. Coupled with the return of the very same pitch class which opened the solo, this moment brings both the last gesture and the entire composition to a striking conclusion.

It is interesting to note that this final tritone is foreshadowed in the lowest tones of the piano part of Gesture 3, where, in the very same register in which the final tuba solo occurs, the piano reiterates the F#-C dyad over and over again:

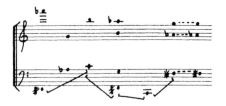

It is important to recall that it was in the third gesture that the piano first introduced the tone C into the composition. It was also in Gesture 3 that the piano assumed the exclusive role of sounding the original trichord as a vertical sonority. Thus, the tone C was first introduced into the composition within the context of the F#, G, A^b cluster. Moreover, it was first introduced as a tritone related to F# which, not by coincidence, is the only tone of the original three carried over into Gesture 4.

In conjunction with the foregoing rather specific analytical observations, it would be revealing to consider some of the composition's more general attributes. One of the most striking characteristics of this piece and, indeed, of Feldman's style in general, is the apparent lack of rhythmic and dynamic articulation. As noted earlier, durations of individual tones are slow but free, and dynamics are constant and quite soft. The result is a very flat surface devoid of any sense of dramatic contrast.

As noted earlier, Feldman's is a music in which there is no apparent structuring of sound prior to its actual unfolding in time. It seems natural, then, that the composer would choose to work within a compositional format in which relationships appear to emerge at the very moment sound is first perceived by the listener and never in any sense prior to that moment; a format in which order never seems imposed by the will of the composer but rather evolves within the perceiver's own awakening consciousness. As such, Feldman avoids all procedures which might tend to reveal his own presence consciously shaping the surface of the music for the listener. With respect to rhythm, for example, he prefers not to *lead* the listener *through* time, but rather to let the listener discover relationships for himself *over* time. In this regard, his music reveals a particular affinity with the philosophy of Heidegger, for central to the work of both men is the notion that understanding is an activity born of time and that, as Heidegger notes: "Being and time determine each other reciprocally..."[11]

The structure of *Durations III, #3* embraces the entire process wherein order is engendered by the appropriation of raw matter. Over the course of the composition a single sonority is first atomized, then extended and finally given meaning as one element within an organized complex of

45

related sounds. From its initial stasis, the music proceeds at an ever increasing pace to reconstruct one basic sonority in a plethora of new formations. As these gradually rise to the fore, the original sound, their source, slowly recedes into the background. From the undifferentiated situation which opens the piece, a rather complex foreground/background hierarchy emerges. In a sense, this is a music born at its conclusion rather than its inception. As the work opens, the listener finds himself poised as if at the brink of his first contact with the world. Later, as relationships gradually coalesce, they appear to do so, not through any act of the composer, but rather through the will of the perceiving consciousness. Along with painters such as Pollock and Rothko and poets like Olson and Creeley, Feldman intensifies the perceiver's awareness of his own role in the formation of a meaningful aesthetic experience. Through such art the perceiver becomes an extension of the artist - a collaborator in the creative act. His consciousness acquires greater definition through the appropriation of the artwork as, simultaneously and reciprocally, the work itself seems to take shape through an act of his will.

1. Charles Olson, *The Special View of History*, Ann Charters, ed. (Berkeley, California: Oyez, 1970), p. 49.

2. Robert von Hallberg, *Charles Olson: The Scholar's Art* (Cambridge, Massachusetts: Harvard University Press, 1978), p. 73.

3. Charles Olson, *The Maximus Poems* (New York: Jargon/Corinth Books, 1960), p. 2.

4. Maurice Merleau-Ponty, *The Primacy of Perception* (Evanston, Illinois: Northwestern University Press, 1964), p. 16.

5. Morton Feldman, *Durations III* (New York: C. F. Peters, 1961), p. 6.

6. Morton Feldman, *Brown/Feldman* (New York: Time Records, No. 58007).

7. Notation of registers: middle C is labeled C^4, the C one octave higher is C^5 and so forth; the C one octave lower is C^3 and so forth. All tones between C^i and C^j, where i and j are adjacent integers, are given the superscript i and so fall within register i.

8. Robert Cogan, Pozzi Escot, *Sonic Design* (Englewood Cliffs, New Jersey: Prentice-Hall, Inc., 1973), p. 356.

9. *Ibid.*, p. 356.

10. 1 = minor 2nd or Major 7th,   2 = Major 2nd or minor 7th,
    3 = minor 3rd or Major 6th,   4 = Major 3rd or minor 6th,
    5 = Perfect 4th or 5th,   6 = tritone.

11. Martin Heidegger, *On Time and Being* (New York: Harper and Row Publishers, 1972), p. 3.

Structure As Behavior

Christian Wolff
For 1, 2 or 3 People

CHRISTIAN WOLFF

Christian Wolff (b. 1934; Nice, France) received a Ph. D. from Harvard in comparative literature and taught classics at that institution for many years. Though largely self-taught in musical composition, he has written numerous articles on contemporary music for such periodicals as *Die Reihe*, *Collage*, *Audience* and *Sonus*. His works are published by C. F. Peters and are recorded on several labels including Composers Recordings, Inc., Wergo, Vox and Mainstream. He is currently a member of the faculties of both the Music and Classics Departments of Dartmouth College in Hanover, New Hampshire.

There is a moment in Ezra Pound's *Pisan Cantos* when the poet
suddenly becomes conscious of both the wooden packing crate on which he
is writing and the person who provided the makeshift table for him:

> In less than a geological epoch
>
> said Henry Mencken
>
> "Some cook, some do not cook,
>
> some things cannot be altered"
>
> Ἰυγξ . . . ᾿εμὸν ποτί δῶμα τὸν ἄνδρα
>
> What counts is the cultural level,
>
> thank Benen for this table ex packing box
>
> "doan yu tell no one I made it"
>
> from a mask as fine as any in Frankfurt
>
> "It'll get you offn th' groun"
>
> Light as the branch of Kuanon
>
> *Canto LXXXI*[1]

Subtly, the reader becomes aware that the act of writing and its object
have fused as the reality of creating the poem becomes enmeshed within
the very fabric of the poem itself. At this moment the poet's thought has
no subject other than its own emergence. The mind recognizes in its appropriation of the world the creation of the self. The poet and the act of
writing - the poet's engagement with the world - become one and the same,
inseparable fragments of a continuum which fuses consciousness, action and
object.

Despite the recurrence of many themes central to the entire series
of cantos, what emerges as predominant in the Pisan collection is the vivid
re-creation of the human thought process. For more than thirty years this
theme has dominated progressive American writing and is addressed with
particular intensity in the works of more recent poets, such as
Jackson MacLow and David Antin, for whom the only subject for poetry is
the very act of speaking. From this theme a new dialectic emerges, one
having to do not so much with a perceiver/object dualism, but with the

51

process of perception and the way in which consciousness becomes manifest by virtue of that process.

This attitude toward the creative act has been central to the development of the visual arts of the past thirty years as well, and is most readily apparent in the works of Bruce Nauman, Robert Morris and Robert Irwin. Throughout the '60's, Nauman worked on a series of pieces in which he used his own body as the "material" upon which he acted. In a 1968 hologram entitled *Making Faces,* the artist used his face as material to be shaped and deformed in various ways. In a work such as this, what is most important is the fact that the object acted upon is the very source of those same actions.

> This concern with the physical self is not simply artistic egocentrism, but use of the body to transform intimate subjectivity into objective demonstration. Man is the perceiver and the perceived; he acts and is acted upon; he is the sensor and the sensed. His behavior constitutes a dialectical interchange with the world he occupies.[2]

Eventually, Nauman shifted focus away from his own body toward those of others. As the artist has noted with respect to the first of his corridor pieces:

> I began to think about how you relate to a particular place, which I was doing by pacing around [referring to the film of himself pacing around his studio in a large square]...then I began thinking about how to present this *without making a performance,* so that somebody else would have the same experience instead of just having to watch me (or anyone else) having that experience...
>
> The earliest pieces were just narrow corridors. The first one I used was a prop for a

52

piece that was taped. It was presented as a prop for a performance and was called that, without any description of what the performance was.

It was just a very narrow grey corridor and all you could do was walk in and walk out. It limited the kinds of things you could do...because I don't like the idea of free manipulation, of putting a bunch of stuff out there and letting people do what they want with it. I really had more specific kinds of experiences in mind...[3]

In this work, entitled *Performance Corridor* (1968), the viewer becomes both the subject and object of his own experience. Although earlier works were experienced by observing the artist functioning as performer, here the artist constructs the piece in such a way that the viewer must activate it for himself. The corridor is an exceptionally narrow space rarely encountered in everyday activities. At the same time, it is a highly directed space. One can only move in two directions and, since the walls are too high to see over, one can only see in those same two directions. Thus, vision is linked with mobility. The artwork leads the perceiver to an understanding of the operations of his own physical being. Moreover, "because most of the...corridors...are designed for one person at a time to enter, it would appear that the audience has been dispensed with, forcing the solitary spectator into a carefully manipulated behavioral pattern *that does not signify anything*."[4] Nauman has not re-created any quality of his own experience of such a space. The viewer must traverse it and experience it for himself. The artwork transcends its traditional role as an object invested with meaning and becomes the occasion for pure consciousness.

It is precisely this point of externalizing the experience of art which links Nauman's work to that of Christian Wolff. One of the most striking aspects of Wolff's music and the central issue guiding the development of his innovative notation is the tacit recognition that the morphology of form is nothing more, nor less, than a resonance of the structure of human behavior. With remarkable precision, he identifies those aspects of physical existence which constitute human experience and makes the perceiver aware that the nature of human behavior is:

> ...neither a series of blind reactions to external 'stimuli' nor the projection of acts which are motivated by the pure ideas of a disembodied, worldless mind. It is neither exclusively subjective nor exclusively objective but a dialectical interchange between man and the world...It is a circular dialectic in which independent beings of the life field, already selected by the structure of the human body, exert a further selective operation on the body's acts. It is out of this dialectical interchange that human meanings emerge.[5]

Through his music Wolff seems to contend that: "Meanings are neither passively assimilated from an external order...as the realists have imagined, nor constructed 'de novo' by a creative mind as the idealists have supposed."[6] Instead, he identifies the gestures of behavior with the forms issuing therefrom and, ultimately, with the appropriation of meaning.

These attitudes first become apparent in Wolff's pieces from the early '60's such as the *Duo for Violinist and Pianist* (1961) and the string quartet, *Summer* (1961). However, even these pieces preserve some vestige of the historical separation of object from action as certain parameters, in particular, pitch and timbre, are still fixed precompositionally. Thus, Wolff maintains a certain degree of control over each composition's unfolding. The composer's ideas and notation crystallize in later works such as *For 1, 2 or 3 People* (1964) and *Edges* (1968).

For 1, 2 or 3 People is indeterminate with respect to all sonic parameters and any specific morphological propensity. The score consists of ten separate sheets one of which, the third, is reproduced on the following page. These may be utilized to make a performance in one of two

54

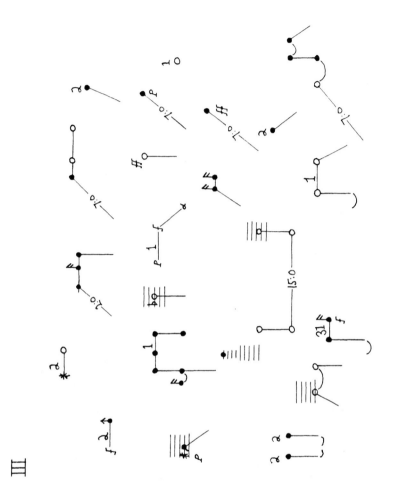

ways: first, any number of sheets may be played in any order without repetition; or, second, one sheet may be repeated as often as desired up to ten times. One, two or three people may perform, using any instruments. Further instructions read, in abridgement, as follows:

> Play all that is notated on a page, in any convenient sequence, not repeating anything...
>
> Black notes are variously short, up to about one second. With stems as sixteenth notes they are very short. White notes are of any length, sometimes determined by the requirements of coordination...
>
> A diagonal line towards a note = play that note directly after a preceding one. A diagonal line away from a note = that note must be followed directly by another.
>
> A vertical line down from a note = play simultaneously with the next sound (both attack and release)...
>
> If a line to a note is broken by a number followed, after a colon, by a zero (-2:0-)...that number of seconds of silence intervene before the required coordination.

                = play after a previous sound has begun, hold until it stops.

                = start anytime, hold till another sound starts, finish with it.

                = start at the same time (or as soon as you are aware of it) as the next sound, but stop before it does.

                = start anytime, hold till another sound starts, continue holding anytime after that sound has stopped.

> Horizontal lines joining two notes = a legato from the one to the other...

Larger numbers on a line between notes:
if black = that number of changes of some
aspect(s) of the sound before reaching the next
note; in red = that number of changes of the
timbre of the first note before reaching the
next one...

↑ = high in some aspect.[7]

Thus, for instance, the first symbol on the upper left side of page III,

$$f \underline{\quad 2 \quad} ↑$$

directs the performer: first, to play any loud sound; then, while holding
that sound, to change two aspects of it (perhaps volume and timbre); and,
finally, to move to another sound which is high in some way. In contrast,
the symbol near the lower right corner of the page,

directs the performer to play his first sound only after he hears one of the
other players produce a sound. He is to hold his sound until the other stops,
ending as close as possible to it. In addition, while holding his sound he is
instructed to change one aspect of its character (for instance, it might get
louder or softer). After this first gesture is completed, he is to move
directly and smoothly to another pitch which is itself to be followed by one
more sound produced by himself or any one of the other players.

Any analysis of *For 1, 2 or 3 People* should begin with John Cage's
observations concerning the nature of Wolff's music:

...the division of the whole into parts is indeterminate. Method, the note-to-note procedure, is
also indeterminate. [And]...the morphology of
the continuity, is unpredictable...*It is not a time
object but rather a process.*[8]

First, one must deduce aspects of its morphology which characterize and
direct the specific type of process which is its structure. As noted above, a

performance may be devised in one of two ways, either by playing several pages in any order or by repeating one page a number of times. Thus, the performers are given a great deal of flexibility in determining the degree of focus desired and where that focus might be placed. The first option provides a large repertory of gestures which, in diverse ways, influence the interaction among the participants. The latter is more limited, forcing each performer continually to discover new and varied uses for a very small number of gestures. Though the repertory of movements may be quite small, a performance designed in this way can reveal multiple facets of each gesture as they constantly reappear in ever changing and totally unpredictable contexts.

Each symbol or set of interconnected symbols is scattered randomly about a page and may be performed in any order. Since the composer is only concerned with coordinating responses to actions which are themselves not predetermined, the process is, of necessity, non-linear. Order is determined solely by the contiguity of events. A symbol is used when it is appropriate, either because it is applicable or desirable. If a performer's actions are to be triggered by those of another he must wait until the appropriate moment to begin. If he is to initiate sound on his own, he may simply act, ignoring all consequences and potential, unpredictable resonances. Throughout, context determines the succession of events.

It is important to recognize, however, that freedom of choice is often quite limited. In all but one case (page IX) the symbols on a given sheet may be played only once. Thus, as one begins a particular page, one has a great deal of freedom of choice and flexibility in terms of the initiation of action or the range of responses available to another's actions. As one proceeds through the page, however, one's freedom becomes more and more constrained; one's ability to respond more limited until, eventually, a point of stasis may be reached where either one can no longer act or has no choice as to which gestures to employ. In the latter case the gestures are, *de facto*, fixed in a specific temporal order.

As is typical of many of Wolff's compositions of this period, three types of activities are notated: activities which initiate sounds; activities which coordinate sounds; and, activities which transform sounds. Of these, the second type is by far the most common and most significant in this work.[9] Actions which initiate sounds function primarily as catalysts for occasional changes in movement while gestures of transformation afford the opportunity to extend or enrich an individual part. In addition, the composer employs a variety of modifyers which restrict the amount of choice the performers are given in realizing each of the three types of symbols when they appear in the score.

Of the first type of activity - that which initiates sound - there is one basic notation:

X = any sound

The composer also employs two modifiers which restrict the type of sound which may be produced:

O = pitched sound

✹ = noise

As stated above, the activities of coordination are the most abundant and richly varied of any employed in this piece. Of these there are basically two types: those which designate temporal coordination and those which represent some other type of coordination. The former are far more common in the piece and indeed in Wolff's music in general. There are two basic gestures which organize sound temporally:

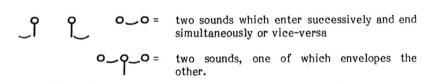

<table>
<tr><td></td><td>= two simultaneous sounds</td></tr>
<tr><td></td><td>= two successive sounds</td></tr>
</table>

The composer combines them in a variety of ways which render coordination more specific:

O⌣O = two sounds which enter successively and end simultaneously or vice-versa

O⌣O⌣O = two sounds, one of which envelopes the other.

In addition, there are several symbols which suggest other levels of interaction and which appear infrequently:

59

⊖ = a sound which is in some respect "in a middle place" vis-a-vis the sounds around it, for example a tone which is in the middle of all sounding registers

△ = a sound which is in some respect "dissonant" with those sounds which precede it

⊕ = a sound which is in some respect "as far away as possible" from the sounds which precede it.

Finally, there are the gestures of transformation. These allow each performer to expand his own part with or without coordination. They include:

___x___ = (where x = any integer) a certain number of changes in some aspect of the sound; if the number is red those changes must be made with respect to the timbre of the sound

〜 = any slight alteration of a sound

∧ = cut off a sound

⟶ = extend a sound

⟋ = raise a sound in some respect

⟍ = lower a sound in some respect

ᒣ = change in spatial location.

The composer frequently limits the amount of choice he allows each performer in realizing the symbols. The following *modifiers* help specify the type of sound to be produced:

time: ● = short

♪ = very short

as fast = as fast as possible
asp

register: ↑ = high in some aspect

↓ = low in some aspect

color: ◊ =   harmonic
                  w =   wood
               met =   metal
                pl =   plucking
                etc.

and intensity: pp through fff.

Large numbers placed over a note specify the number of tones or timbres to be played.

Certain modifiers restrict the gestures of coordination by pinpointing the exact moments of coordination rather than leaving them up to the performer's choice. The symbol

$$\text{?}$$

which specifies no particular point of connection is rendered more precise as

   x = 2,   coordinate with the second sound which follows
   x = 3,   coordinate with the third sound which follows
   etc.

while

$$\text{/} \qquad \text{\\}$$

are rendered more precise as

   x = 2,   coordinate with the second sound which follows
   x = 3,   coordinate with the third sound which follows
   etc.

In addition, he frequently introduces silence in order to give a more precise timing to the succession of tones.

$$\text{/} \qquad \text{\\}$$

are rendered more precise as

   x = 2,   insert two seconds of silence before
              completing the required coordination
   x = 3,   insert three seconds of silence.

The syntax which governs Wolff's structure incorporates the three fundamental components of his language of actions - initiation, coordination and transformation - in a rich and varied array of formations. This syntax may be discerned in any single instrumental part:

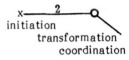

initiation
transformation
coordination

or in a combination of parts, as when coordination is required for initiation:

player
1

player
2

Syntax, however, is not ordered in time. For example, coordination may come first:

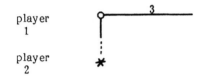

Each page of the score is characterized by different syntactic formations which are unique in structure and yield a different complex of interactions. The gesture most characteristic of page III is

7:0

which is distinguished by a rather lengthy delay before coordinated is effected. It is presented in several variations:

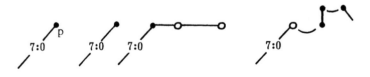

7:0   7:0   7:0   7:0

The first two fix, somewhat, the duration and volume of the connected tone. The third and fourth extend that tone to other pitches of variable duration, while the fourth effects further extension by linking up with other symbols.

In contrast, there are two very distinctive gestures of coordination which characterize page IV. The first is

a single tone of variable duration, intensity, color and frequency which ends with any sound the performer hears or produces. While this type of gesture appears only two times on the third page, it appears nine times on the fourth where it is presented in two basic forms. The first fixes the end point of the sound (the point of connection between sounds) in three different ways, the second of which appears twice:

The second specifies the type of sound to be made as well as, occasionally, the end point:

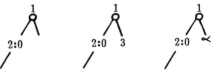

The second type of gesture which characterizes page IV is itself a variant on the one that characterized page II, since it too delays coordination:

This gesture appears in three forms, the second of which also appears twice:

In these respects, the third and fourth pages differ quite sharply with one another. They differ even more, however, with the first two pages which contained no such timed connections.

Other factors which characterize a given page have to do with the use of gestures which require no coordination. In general, these are used quite sparsely. On the third page, for instance, of the twenty-two symbols employed, only two require no coordination:

With respect to the fourth page, the situation is quite similar. Of the thirty-four symbols employed only four require no coordination:

In contrast, on the very first page, of the twenty-seven gestures employed, one-third require no coordination. Page I, then, is characterized by much less coordinated activity than either pages III or IV - or any others for that matter.

In listening to this music, one is struck by the fact that several renderings of the same notated gesture rarely, if ever, produce patterns which are recognizably similar. "The complexities of this notation are directed less at an arrangement of sounds resulting from the performer's actions than at the conditions under which their actions are to be produced."[10] Thus, the notated symbols never determine any particular melodic contour nor any other specific type of sonic configuration. All that is ever defined symbolically is a complex of interactions among the performers. As Wolff has explained: "People sometimes ask, why don't you just specify what you want and be done with it? I do! Actions are indicated..."[11]

What one hears are the gestures themselves, gestures which are usually taken for granted as the means to an end, but which are here drawn out as an end in themselves. Thus, for example, the idea of playing together takes on importance as an act in itself. Each performance is guided by carefully manipulated behavioral patterns which do not generate products and, as such, do not signify anything beyond their essential characterization as behavior. In this music, one ceases to distinguish between signs and signifiers - forms and the behavior which engenders such forms. The work is not so much a construction of sound as a situation of action and response defined abstractly through sound. What is perceived as form is the ensemble of these interactions while the aural result is merely one particular sonic projection of that form. That "dialectical interchange" by which form and meaning are engendered is, in this music, embodied within the very substance of its audible structure.

It is significant that, of the activities which Wolff has notated, the vast majority are activities of coordination. In his works actions are intimately tied to responses. In fact, by and large, the actions are themselves responses. In this way the composer identifies the notions of action and response as inseparable. Actions are themselves responses which, in turn, generate further responses from others. Acting affects and is, at the same time, affected. As expressed by Merleau-Ponty:

> The enigma is that my body simul-
> taneously sees and is seen. That which looks at
> all things can also look at itself and recognize,
> in what it sees, the 'other side' of its power of
> looking. It sees itself seeing; touches itself
> touching; it is visible and sensitive for itself. It
> is not a self through transparence, like thought,
> which only thinks its object by assimilating it,
> by constituting it, by transforming it into
> thought. It is a self through confusion, narcis-

65

sism through inherence of the one who sees in that which he sees and through inherence of sensing in the sensed...[12]

As does Nauman with his "corridor" pieces, Wolff also shifts the focus of his artwork away from his own experience to that of the performer. In *For 1, 2 or 3 People* he externalizes the creative process itself. He distills the essential components of behavior and frees them from the subjugation of his own personal taste, leading the performer and, ultimately, the perceiver to a conscious awareness of his actions under diverse conditions. In a sense, in this music, the performer becomes his own *object trouvé*; the subject of his discourse is the mechanism of that discourse. What is revealed, then, are the ways in which patterns of behavior shape human experience. By abstracting the artist's actions from the creative process, Wolff transforms the artwork into a metaphor for the physical embodiment and expression of meaning which is both fundamental to, and inseparable from, the process of being in the world.

1. Ezra Pound, *The Cantos* (New York: New Directions Books, 1948), pp. 518-519.

2. Carla Gottlieb, *Beyond Modern Art* (New York: E. P. Dutton and Co., 1976), p. 256-257.

3. Bruce Nauman quoted by Jane Livingston, "Bruce Nauman" in *Bruce Nauman, Work from 1965-72* (Los Angeles: Los Angeles County Museum of Art, 1972), p. 42.

4. Marcia Tucker, "Bruce Nauman" in *Bruce Nauman, Work from 1965-72* (Los Angeles: Los Angeles County Museum of Art, 1972), p. 42.

5. John Wild, forward to *The Structure of Behavior*, Maurice Merleau-Ponty (Boston: Beacon Press, 1967), p. xiv.

6. *Ibid.*, p. xv.

7. Christian Wolff, *For 1, 2 or 3 People* (New York: C. F. Peters, 1964), p. 1.

8. John Cage, *Silence* (Middletown, Connecticut: Wesleyan University Press, 1961), pp. 38-39.

9. In contrast one might consider a work such as *Edges* (1968) which is concerned primarily with gestures of initiation.

10. David Behrman, "What Indeterminate Notation Determines" in *Perspectives on Notation and Performance*, Benjamin Boretz and Edward Cone, eds. (New York: W. W. Norton Co., 1976), p. 89.

11. Christian Wolff, *John Cage/Christian Wolff* (Mainstream Records, MS 5015).

12. Maurice Merleau-Ponty, "Eye and Mind" in *The Primacy of Perception* (Evanston, Illinois: Northwestern University Press, 1964), pp. 162-163.

Structural Pluralism

Robert Ashley
in memoriam . . . Esteban Gomez

ROBERT ASHLEY

Robert Ashley (b. 1930; Ann Arbor, Michigan) attended the University of Michigan where he studied composition and acoustics and the Manhattan School of Music where he majored in piano and composition. In 1969 he became director of the Mills College Center for Contemporary Music in Oakland California, a position which he held until 1981. He has written articles for the *Tulane Drama Review, Arts in Society* and *Source*. His complete works are published by Visibility Music Publishers and several recent music/theater works are recorded on Lovely Music/Vital Records. He currently resides in New York City where he performs on a regular basis.

In a recent essay on structuralism, Jean Piaget proposed the following definition: "As a first approximation we may say that a structure is a system of transformations."[1] What is significant about this definition is the emphasis placed on the concept of transformation as the foundation upon which all structure is built. Moreover, it proposes that the very elements of structure are themselves activities.

The most progressive new art has continually challenged the notion that the creative process is a form of activity which necessarily results in a unique finished product. As sculptor Robert Morris has noted: "What is revealed [by many new works] is that art is an activity of change."[2] In their desire to articulate this concern, many contemporary artists have striven to identify the structure of their works with the variety of perceptual and constructive processes which constitute the foundation of all creative activity. In Morton Feldman's view:

> What music rhapsodizes in today's 'cool' language is its own construction. The fact that men like Boulez and Cage represent opposite extremes of modern methodology is not what is interesting. What is interesting is their similarity. In the music of both men what is heard is indistinguishable from its process. In fact, process itself might be called the Zeitgeist of our age.[3]

While one may argue, with good reason, that the differences are also important, Feldman's comments are significant.

The twentieth century has witnessed the emergence of an increased awareness that structure can no longer be viewed simply as a family of relationships discerned among the elements of a single closed gestalt. Rather, a structure is a complex process evolving over a period of time, integrating an elaborate and diverse range of activities reaching out far beyond the framework of the art object itself. It is a continuum of activities beginning with a series of perceptions and proceeding through a network of interrelated transformations. Such recent concepts of structure have extended the traditional view of the fixed art object to include, as active ingredients in the very form of the work itself, all the activities of either a perceptual or constructive nature invoked by the artist in the course of its creation. This expanded notion of structure has had at least two significant consequences. First, it has tied the finished artwork back to the sources of its evolution and has clearly articulated those sources within the structure of the artwork; and, second, it has exposed the nature of the process by which those sources are tied to that finished product.

The attitude that form may be identified with an organic growth process is clearly demonstrated in Richard Serra's well known series of "lead splash" sculptures. In *Casting* (1969), for instance, hot, liquified lead was drawn in a ladle and thrown into the juncture formed by the wall and floor planes of a gallery room. This action was repeated many times. As the lead hardened, a thin crust of metal formed along the side of the room. When finished, the lead shape was removed. This process was repeated several times, resulting in a set of similarly shaped lead casts. The last cast was left in place along the side of the room while the others were turned over and lined up on the floor parallel to the juncture against which they were made.

In this work all the activities of construction are invoked with tremendous immediacy in at least three significant ways. First, within each individual lead cast, one can discern the residue of both the hurling action and the mold against which that action was directed. The underside of each cast is relatively smooth, and its angle neatly shaped by the wall and floor planes. On top in contrast, clearly visible on the cast left right-side-up, a very rough surface texture reflects the nature and energy of the hurling and splashing actions. In addition, it shows that these actions were repeated many times leading up to the emergence of the final shape.

Second, the act of lining up several of these casts focuses even more clearly on the work's making process, suggesting, on a much larger scale, the idea of generating form through the repetition of a single gesture.

Through this simple serial ordering procedure, the artist isolates and focuses on the all-important gesture of repetition from among those available to him within his original set of actions.

Third, the decision to leave one cast in place brings into the visible sphere of the piece the mold from which the shapes were formed. The mold thus becomes as much a part of the means of production as the hurling action. The piece appears frozen at the instant of its completion – at the moment when the final cast is taking shape. This is yet another way in which the artist vividly invokes the methodology of creating.

Finally, it is interesting to note the double meaning in the title *Casting*. "Casting" may refer to either a throwing action or to an object fashioned by pouring liquid into a mold. One often encounters works created through this traditional procedure, but in such cases, the result is a sculptured image which in no way reflects the pouring action employed. In fact, once the cast is formed, the mold is discarded. In Serra's work, however, both the throwing gesture and the mold are clearly visible within the sculpture. The sculptured "image" is not really an image at all; it is the reflection of an activity and of the mechanisms used in carrying out that activity. Even the work's title suggests a fusion of process and form. In *Casting* the viewer not only experiences the finished product but also the dynamic processes of emergence and assembly as they were experienced by the artist himself. Its structure cannot be understood apart from its making process.

One significant consequence of such an intense identification of a form with its morphology is that the catalysts for this process are drawn to the surface of the artwork. Any work's structure may be understood as the result of a vital interaction between a particular context and a specific style of behavior; every process is rooted in certain materials and in the potential of those materials for transformation. As the philosopher Merleau-Ponty notes: "Matter is pregnant with form."[4] Any material engenders a particular range of gestures by which it may be transformed. This range is determined by both the specific physical constitution of the particular type of matter employed and the referential constraints imposed on the use of that material by all other materials employed in the composition. With respect to the first point, one need only refer to the sculpture just discussed. Lead is a metal which can be melted into some liquid form and then thrown against a wall where it will harden rather quickly. In contrast, wood does not lend itself to this kind of manipulation. Clearly, a material suggests the actions by which it may be altered, shaped or otherwise transformed in ways germane to its own physical constitution. The choice of specific materials to some degree determines the limits and general nature of any structure into which those materials may be fashioned.

Once a context has been determined and relevant transforming gestures suggested, choices are made as to the nature of the transformations which are to take place. Such choices reflect the artist's style, his characteristic way of dealing with materials. Robert Morris' comments on this subject are revealing:

> Objects project possibilities for actions as much as they themselves project that they were acted upon; the former allows for subtle identifications and orientations; the latter if emphasized is a recovery of the time that welds together ends and means...[5]

> The body's activities as it engages in manipulating various materials according to different processes has open to it different possibilities for behavior. What the hand, arms and body can do in relation to a flat surface is different from what hand, arms and body movement can do in relation to objects in three dimensions. Such differences of engagement (and their extension of technological means) amount to different forms of behavior.[6]

Thus, context and style interact with one another in a variety of ways to evolve structure.

The intense focus which contemporary art has placed upon the making process has quite naturally brought these sources of structural evolution to the forefront of the viewer's attention. In the case of Serra's *Casting*, any understanding of the sculpture's structure·ultimately centers upon the conscious recognition of the physical properties of lead, the type of human activity relevant to the transformation of that material, and the specific activities from among all those available which were employed by the artist in creating the piece.

This shift of emphasis away from the end product of the creative process, first toward the process itself and then toward the generative sources of that process, leads to several observations, all of which are central to any study of open structure in contemporary art and music. As stated above, any specific context will suggest certain relevant transforming gestures, or operations, germane to its physical nature, and any style will choose and direct those operations in ways germane to its particular and unique sensibilities. This would suggest that each process is to some extent unique. The traditional closed artwork is then the singular product of an interaction between specific materials and one specific style. Herein lies the source of its closed nature.

It would seem, therefore, that it is with respect to these two catalytic aspects of any morphological scheme - its materials and style - that openness may be introduced into structure. Clearly, if one or both of these components were left undefined throughout the evolution of an artwork, a radically new orientation toward form would emerge. In particular, the removal of any specific definition of context or materials from the process of creating a sonic or visual structure opens up the possibility of creating an artwork which is itself a process determined without reference to any specific end product; a structure which is a reflection of the pure mechanism of process.

In this respect it is important to note that, despite its intense identification of form with morphology, *Casting* is, in the end, a fixed art object. In contrast, the work of composer Robert Ashley represents an approach to composition which rejects completely the idea that the

75

creative act need end with the construction of any such final product. While reinforcing the attitude toward structure exemplified in the work of an artist such as Richard Serra, Ashley embraces a concept of indeterminacy which intensifies the perception of structure as an activity of change.

Robert Ashley's composition *in memoriam...Esteban Gomez* vividly demonstrates this point. The work is a quartet for any combination of instruments. The score is graphic and is presented below:

The instructions read as follows:

> The graph is read circularly. Each dot represents a constant unit of time that is determined privately by each performer. This unit should be a natural pulse that does not tend to subdivide in the performer's mind.
>
> The individual performer assigns to each quadrant of the score one of the following sound elements: *pitch; intensity; timbre*; density***.

---

*   "timbre" refers to tonal color changes effected through the use of mutes, filters, bow movement, etc.
**   "density" refers to the mixing of tonal ingredients, as in flutter-tongue, double-stops, mixed vocal and instrumental sound, etc.

These sound elements may be assigned to the quadrants in any pattern, and that pattern - while it will "revolve" in its relationship to the score - will remain constant (in the relationship of its parts) throughout the performance.

The ensemble should prepare a sonority within which the individual instruments are not distinguishable. This sonority will provide, for the individual performers, a tonal reference for the various sound activities that constitute the performance.

Whenever any performer is playing his contribution to the reference sonority, time (duration) is unmeasured (free) for him.

Whenever any performer is playing through the (16) measured pulses of a quadrant, he must deviate continuously, but as gradually as possible, from his contribution to the reference sonority.

The performance begins with the reference sonority. At any time, then, individual performers may play through any (starting) quadrant. Subsequently, they will continue reading circularly, alternating unmeasured periods of their contribution to the reference sonority with measured periods of assigned deviations.

Whenever any performer first becomes aware of a deviant element (other than his own) in the reference sonority, his pattern of assigned sound elements (quadrants) shifts circularly so that the mode of deviation he recognizes is assigned to the quadrant opposite that in which he is playing or will play next. (As the pattern of quadrants remains constant, thus, all quadrants will be redesignated.) The pattern of quadrant designations remains in its changed position until the performer has played through the succeeding (newly designated) quadrant, after which it is subject again to transposition through the appearance of the deviant elements in the sonority.[7]

The work is to be performed by any four instruments. This quartet prepares a "reference sonority"; a particular sound which will serve as the central unifying element of the composition and the source of all sonic activity. It is in this sense a reference point in the compositional process for both the performer and the listener: for the performer, it is the starting point from which he may evolve a structure and to which he must constantly return over the course of this evolution; for the listener, it is the background against which he understands all the compositional activity which takes place.

The reference sonority is a sound within which the individual instruments are not distinguishable. Certainly many such reference sonorities can be imagined for any particular quartet. For example, some might consist of soft, sustained attackless sounds. Many instruments lose their unique identifying tone quality and approach that of a sine tone in such a situation and so become rather hard to identify. Other reference sonorities might consist of dense, active masses of sound tightly packed within one register. Here the total sonority would approach white noise and, once again, it would be difficult for the ear to distinguish the individual components of the sound. Also, sonorities might be conceived within which masking would be used to render the individual components indistinguishable. These are only a few of the various possibilities that, in addition, may be combined in different ways to achieve the desired result.

The instruction for gradual deviation from this sound may also be interpreted in a variety of ways. As it is to be applied to each of the four sonic parameters listed in the score, examples will be given which treat each parameter in turn. These examples have been composed for the violin. It will be assumed that this instrument's contribution to a reference sonority is A^4, bowed, played softly, and repeated every half note at = 60:

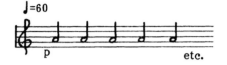

Gradual deviation with respect to each parameter may be interpreted in the following ways:

pitch

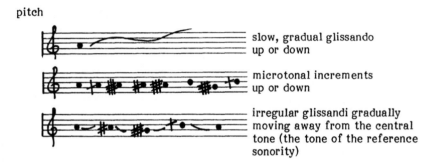

slow, gradual glissando up or down

microtonal increments up or down

irregular glissandi gradually moving away from the central tone (the tone of the reference sonority)

density

sing and play in unison

Bartok pizz.

timbre

In the following examples n=arco normale, sp=arco sul ponticello (½ or ¼sp refer to relative distance toward bridge), st=arco sul tasto, clt=col legno tratto.

→ means gradual change from one timbre to another.

○　○　○　○　○　○　　○　○
n→⅓sp→n→⅓sp ⅓st→n →sp →n

○　○　○　○　○　○
n →⅓sp ⅓st→sp →st→ n

intensity

♩ ♩ ♩ ♩ ♩ ♩ ♩ ♩
p ⟨mp⟩pp ⟨⟨mf⟩ pp ⟨f⟩ppp

The instruction to always deviate gradually from the norm is quite significant. It ensures that all transformation of the sonic materials of the piece, the reference sonority, will be gradual and so always be heard as rooted in, and growing from, those materials. All change is, then, understood as emerging from one common source. Were the composer to allow sudden or abrupt transformations, their source might be lost. This is one way in which the composer ensures the constant aural presence of the reference sonority throughout any performance. Since all transformations are heard as gradual outgrowths of this sound, its presence will always be invoked.

Another instruction, however, goes even further to ensure this continuing presence. In the score, a circle is divided by four large dots into four quadrants, each of which is subdivided by smaller dots into sixteen parts. To each quadrant is assigned, independently by each performer, one of the four sonic parameters to be transformed in the course of any performance. For example, one performer might label the quadrants in the following manner:

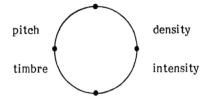

The large dots represent unmeasured periods of time in which each performer plays his unaltered contribution to the reference sonority. These alternate with periods in which the performer departs from the large dot moving either clockwise or counterclockwise through one of the two surrounding quadrants. The sixteen parts of that quadrant represent sixteen equal time segments. The duration of each segment is to be chosen freely by each performer and for each quadrant each time it is played. This series of sixteen equal durations serves as a background against which the deviations may be carried out, measuring their progress in whatever way the performer chooses. The deviations themselves are to be applied to whichever parameter has been assigned to the quadrant chosen for performance at that moment.

More specifically, any performance begins with all four players on a large dot, not necessarily the same one, producing for some undetermined period of time the reference sonority. Presumably, it would be helpful if this sound were held for a somewhat lengthy period of time so as to attune the audience to its qualities and importance. The length of time required will then, at least in part, depend on the nature of the sonority chosen. Next, each performer at a moment of his or her own choosing moves off the large dot into a measured period of gradual deviation through some sonic parameter. Since the large dot chosen as the starting point may be different for each performance, and since the direction of motion around the circle may be chosen freely and independently by each performer at any given moment, the parameter subjected to transformation will probably be different for most of the instrumentalists.

Significantly, concerning these movements, Ashley adds the following note to the score:

Whenever any performer first becomes aware of

a deviant element (other than his own) in the
reference sonority, his pattern of assigned
sound elements (quadrants) shifts circularly so
that the mode of deviation he recognizes is
assigned to the quadrant opposite that in which
he is playing or will play next. (As the pattern
of quadrants remains constant, thus, all
quadrants will be redesignated.)[8]

Assuming that a performer has assigned the parameters to the quadrants in
the following manner:

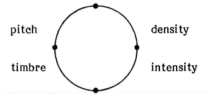

and that he begins on the large dot to the far left, he may then choose to
move through either the pitch or timbre quadrants. As he proceeds through
the chosen quadrant he may begin to hear some other performer altering
his contribution to a different parameter. If, for instance, he proceeds
through the pitch quadrant, he may hear some other performer altering his
contribution to the density of the reference sonority. In other words, as he
plays he hears change in the reference sonority and it is with respect to the
parameter of density that this change is most noticeable to him. He then
changes his mapping of parameters to quadrants circularly (clockwise) so
that the parameter of density is the farthest away from the point on the
graph at which he is now playing. His new "altered" score would look
something like this:

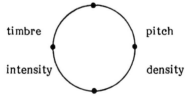

He now continues through the quadrant in which he had been playing, but this time varying his timbre rather than his pitch. Thus, care is taken that he will begin his density deviations only after that other performer has ended his and has returned to his normal density contribution to the reference sonority.

This instruction, then, also ensures the constant presence of the reference sonority. It ensures that no single parameter or even pair of parameters will be transformed by all the performers at the same time, a situation which could possibly result in the severing of all audible ties to that sonority. In following this rule, the deviation will be spread fairly evenly among all the performers and all the parameters. Consequently, at any given moment, a significant portion of the contribution of each parameter to the reference sonority will be heard. Clearly, this action of rotating the assignment of parameters around the graph could easily become cumbersome since a performer will probably always be hearing some change in the reference sonority. To control this activity of rotation, the composer adds the following remarks: "The pattern of quadrant designations remains in its changed position until the performer has played through the succeeding (newly designated) quadrant, after which it is subject again to transposition through the appearance of deviant elements in the sonority."[9] In this way, each performer is also certain to have some lengthy stretches of uninterrupted activity. In two important ways, then, Ashley has ensured the constant presence of the reference sonority. The first is the designation that only gradual deviation be used and the second is the rotation scheme just discussed. Thus, the composer solidifies the function of the main sonority as a truly referential element in the piece.

It would seem that any analysis of this piece must be concerned with two structural levels: the structure of each particular realization of the score and the structure defined by the score alone, that is, the structure which has actually been composed by Ashley himself. For any given realization, two factors are introduced into the work which are not defined by the composer, a specific reference sonority and a particular quartet. These two factors together define the context and the transformation patterns of each realization. With respect to context, the reference sonority presents the sonic materials upon which the structure is based while the four instrumentalists determine the range of possible transformations over that material available during the performance. It should be added that the performers, as well as their instruments, are part of the context since their ability to manipulate those instruments also determines the range of available transformations. The specific transformation patterns utilized in each realization, traditionally the domain of stylistic preference, are here determined by the uniqueness of each performer's imagination and his technical skill. Any performance will be characterized by those patterns and gestures which each performer will naturally tend to use over and over again. Each realization of the score, each performance, results in a unique shape; a particular sonic context evolves into a unique structure. It might be added that the determination of these individual structures is, to some extent, a problem of discovering and defining limits. The cumulative effect of any performance is the determination, or at least suggestion, of some range of deviations or transformations possible, given a specific context and the specific styles of the performers involved. Determining such a range necessitates the discovery of the limits of the ability of each performer and his instrument to transform the specific sonic materials of the realization.

In summary, the actual structure which emerges from each realization is determined by the following factors:

a) the specific quartet and reference sonority chosen;

b) each performer's assignment of parameters to the quadrants;

c) the specific gradual transformations employed;

d) the sequence of transformations determined by each performer's interaction with the others, that is, the circular rotation of the quadrants. The structure of each realization is the resulting network of actual sonic transformations as these occur in time.

It is important to note, however, that a determination of the structure of the entire piece, of all the infinite realizations, must take into

84

account that structure's ability to generate those many different realizations. All that the composer has defined through his score - his graph and his set of instructions - is a very broad procedure for evolving a structure. His style itself has not transformed any materials. Rather, he has removed his style from the work and created a procedure enabling other styles to define a context and evolve a structure. For instance, although Ashley has defined the four sound parameters within which change can take place, these are sufficiently comprehensive as to include just about all the aspects of sonic matter that one could conceive of transforming. The few constraints imposed are themselves very broad. The concept of gradual deviation and the rotation of the quadrants serve to ensure cohesion and to prevent the performance from deteriorating into chaos.

Clearly, since his structure is intended to be adaptable to all materials and styles, he could only define very general guidelines to govern the transformation of sonic matter. Any more specific directions imposed upon the interactive process would reflect Ashley's own style because they would be *his* directions and would necessarily favor certain sonic matter over others. As such, the score would approach a more traditional singular evolution.

The structure of Serra's *Casting*, for instance, was determined by specific transforming operations as they were applied to specific materials and, as mentioned earlier, these operations would not be relevant to just any set of materials. However, if a musical structure is so conceived as to accept any sonic context and to generate a diversity of structures, it must, through its score, suggest only very general indications concerning the transformation of sonic materials. In this way, the composer can introduce a myriad of transforming gestures into the composition's range of activity. Coupling this with the performer's freedom to choose any reference sonority performed by any combination of instruments, one can see that this quartet actually encompasses a multitude of different interactive processes. Ashley has created a work which can accept many unique structures. The specific interactive process between one context and one style found in a more traditional, closed work is here generalized so as to include many such processes. Each performance will be heard and understood as the outgrowth of the specific materials and styles employed.

Of course, the multiplicity engendered by the score would be most apparent after hearing several realizations. It is, however, also suggested within each individual realization. Any performance is the product of an interaction between several performers and certain sonic materials. As such, even within one performance, several distinct styles will become manifest. Within any single realization, the notion of multiplicity will figure quite prominently in that evolutionary process which is the structure of the piece. It is precisely this concern with multiplicity which determines the open nature of the composition.

Ashley's quartet, then, engenders a world of specific structures. His work accepts any context and style and allows, within broad constraints, an apparently endless number of processes to take place. His particular style remains apart from the creative process and is replaced by each individual performer's style. Rather than create a structure which is the result of a specific interaction between himself and some particular sonic material, he has developed a blueprint for such an interaction through which others may create, each in his own way, a particular structure. Thus, it is incorrect to refer to any particular realization of the score as Ashley's composition. Ashley's structure is the framework through which such realizations may evolve. It is the framework for a process yet to be realized. Recognition of this quality of imminence is crucial to any understanding of the work. As noted above, a more traditional, closed structure, such as Serra's *Casting* is really more the document of a completed process, than a process itself. *in memoriam... Esteban Gomez*, however, reveals the very essence of structure, since it is not just the document of a process, it is process itself.

At the beginning of the twentieth century the issue of the uniqueness of each individual creative process seemed to dominate both music and the visual arts. As artists in the nineteenth century eroded the *a priori* conditioning implied by the traditional languages of the various media, attention was focused on the singularity of each individual artwork. The early decades of the twentieth century exploded into a world of multiplicity, the hallmark of which was the definition of form through a materials/style interaction freed from any a priori constraints. As Milton Babbitt has pointed out:

> ...what the dominant composers of [the early decades of the century] shared in common was a lack of, an avoidance of, communality...It was a struggle to create a world of musics, not a struggle between one music and another, serial and non-serial, tonal and a-tonal.[10]

This multiplicity is, in a sense, contained within the limits of Ashley's single composition. Its integration allows not only an extensive exposition of the notion of pluralism, but also reveals, through the composer's understanding of the nature of structure as process, the singular methodology which links much of that diversity which has dominated creative activity in both music and the visual arts thus far in the twentieth century.

1. Jean Piaget, *Structuralism* (New York: Harper Books, 1961), p. 5.

2. Robert Morris, "Some Notes on the Phenomenology of Making" *Artforum* (April, 1970), p. 62.

3. Morton Feldman, quoted by Michael Nyman in *Experimental Music* (New York: Schirmer Books), p.2.

4. Maurice Merleau-Ponty, *The Primacy of Perception* (Evanston, Illinois: Northwestern University Press, 1964), p. 12.

5. Morris, *op. cit.*, p. 66.

6. Morris, *op. cit.*, p. 62

7. Robert Ashley, "in memoriam...Esteban Gomez", *Source* (January, 1967), p. 41.

8. *Ibid.*, p. 41.

9. *Ibid.*, p. 41.

10. Milton Babbitt, "Edgard Varese: A Few Observations On His Music" in *Perspectives on American Composers,* Benjamin Boretz and Edward Cone, eds. (New York: W. W. Norton, 1971), p. 45.

The Shape of Sound

Alvin Lucier
Music for Pure Waves,
Bass Drums and Acoustic Pendulums

ALVIN LUCIER

Alvin Lucier (b. 1931; Nashua, New Hampshire) studied at Yale University and did graduate work at Brandeis where he also taught and directed a chorus noted for its performances of new music. A complete collection of his scores appears in *Chambers*, a book of interviews with Douglas Simon published by Wesleyan University Press. Recordings of his major compositions are available on Lovely Music/Vital Records. He is currently chairman of the Music Department at Wesleyan University in Middletown, Connecticut.

In the introduction to his masterpiece, *Paterson*, William Carlos Williams identified one of the central issues addressed by the avant-garde of the twentieth century: "...no ideas but in things."[1] With this objectivist maxim Williams helped set in motion a line of inquiry which has dominated the most progressive developments in literature, the visual arts and music thus far in the second half of the twentieth century. In turn, this inquiry has led to a major re-evaluation of the nature of human discourse and the forms through which that discourse becomes manifest as art.

Within this body of work, the music of Alvin Lucier holds a crucial position. Continuing the pathbreaking explorations of such innovators as John Cage and Morton Feldman, Lucier became one of the first American composers to eschew all gestural aspects of traditional composition and to replace them with the pure physical presence of sound. Rather than use sound as material to be shaped into some personal utterance, he presents sound in as tactile a physical manifestation as possible. The result is an art which re-creates the very conditions of reality itself.

Clearly, the notion that an artwork need not necessarily evolve from any purposeful shaping or making process has its roots in the seminal works of John Cage. Cage was one of the first musicians to recognize that the purpose of art need not be the expression of its creator's personal definition of reality. Rather, Cage came to realize that art may be used to acknowledge the presence of things - the factness of life - and through this primal act to determine the very meaning of consciousness. His extensive use of chance techniques engendered structures which neither organized sound for some expressive/dramatic purpose nor fashioned it into abstract designs. Instead, Cage simply chose to present sound, and in so doing, forced the listener to become more conscious of its existence and meaning within the horizon of the physical world.

Throughout the '60's and '70's this same concern was, in one way or another, beginning to dominate the work of almost all progressive

91

American artists, writers and composers. In reference to his early minimal paintings, for instance, the visual artist Robert Irwin once remarked: "The thing to realize was that the reduction (involved in these paintings) was a reduction of imagery to get at physicality, *a reduction of metaphor to get at presence.*"[2] For Irwin, the goal was to expurgate all *metaphors* of presence from the experience of art and to replace them with a conscious awareness of perception. In the best experience of this art, the perceiver is located at the very moment his own perceptions become manifest to himself - at the very brink of his first contact with the world. This, in turn, leads to a re-examination of the role of the perceiver in the experience of the artwork as it forces a heightened awareness of the act of perception: "Allowing people to perceive their perceptions...to make people conscious of their consciousness."[3]

Perhaps no other visual artist of the past two decades has been more consistent in addressing these issues than the great sculptor Carl Andre. The rejection of traditional shaping processes in favor of more presentational structures is evident in all his works. *Timbre Piece* (1964), for instance, consists of a simple rectangular construction fashioned from roughly cut pieces of wood arranged in a repeated interlocking pattern. Through the simplicity of the sculpture's shape, the artist succeeds in removing all suggestion of sign-value. The viewer's attention is directed toward the material itself the color, texture and weight of which totally dominate the visual experience. What exists as form - the rectangular shape - merely serves to contain matter and present it in a rather compact format for the viewer's inspection. Moreover, in this sculpture (and perhaps for the first time in Andre's work), the floor plane becomes a dynamic component of the visual structure. The object's massive weight seems to press downward with intensity toward the ground beneath it. The floor becomes a presence which actively engages the sculpture and helps determine its boundaries. In addition, the floor plane tends to focus even more attention upon materials. For Andre, the most natural place for materials to exist and be themselves is close to the ground.

Horizontally is what we know - is what is

here; if sculpture rises in space, it runs the risk
of becoming just an artificial construction
whose very structure takes on more importance
- as a sign - than the fact of the sculpture
itself.[4]

Verticality imposes shape upon materials. Even if only through the most basic gestures of rising into space, it draws attention away from materials and places it, instead, upon the forms into which those materials have been fashioned. As such, verticality is avoided by Andre because it tends to attribute a sense of purpose to the use of materials and renders them subservient to the expression of the artist's personal aesthetic impulses.

In subsequent works, Andre focuses exclusively on non-terminal, serial arrangements resting on the floor. In each of these pieces, repetition provides a simple format within which to present materials in a natural, untouched state. Many are long, thin, low constructions which hug the ground: bricks lined up on the floor in a gallery room; bales of hay at the edge of a forest; logs on the earth near some buildings. Most remarkable, however, is a series of square metal plate pieces dating from the late '60's. In these Andre employs an unobtrusive arrangement of small, very thin, square metal plates laid out on the floor in one large square. Here the need for order is accommodated by repetition and self-reflection. Materials are never shaped in any way but rather are contained and put on display. Moreover, the plates are constructed from a number of metals - zinc, copper, lead, magnesium - the sheer variety of which further directs the perceiver away from form and toward materials. Clearly, the method of this art lies more in the act of presentation than in any type of manipulation or transformation. The result is an intense focus upon presence; the presence of the object to the perceiver which is made vivid through the appropriation of unformed matter.

In Lucier's case, the desire to project sound as pure physical essence seems to have arisen in reaction to certain concepts of gesture and design which had dominated western art through the first half of the twentieth century. With remarkable clarity, the composer himself pinpoints the very

93

moment in his career when this new approach to composition began to emerge. Upon leaving college in 1960, Lucier went to Italy on a Fulbright scholarship:

> My first project in Europe was to be a sonata for small trumpet and harpsichord...My intention was to write a set of variations on a theme of Monteverdi. For some time I had been attracted to the charming echo-duets between pairs of oboes and violins which appear in the *Deposuit* of the *Magnificat* of the *Vespers of 1610* and I planned to base my sonata on this material. Perhaps it was that the disparity between the blown and plucked sounds of the trumpet and harpsichord...made the illusion of echoes impossible...but my enthusiasm for the project soon sputtered and I stopped working.[5]

Sometime later, in one of the first works of his mature style - significantly, a work entitled *Vespers* - actual sonic echoes were used by performers to aid them in moving about a room or concert hall. With the help of special equipment, the performers were able to locate themselves in physical space using processes of echolocation not unlike those of bats or other nocturnal creatures.

> It wasn't until several years later that it struck me that this work was the finished version of the little trumpet sonata that I had begun and abandoned in Venice years before. The title should have told me sooner. Now, however, the echoes are real, not symbolic. They exist in physical space; *they don't have to stand for anything else.*[6]

As was the case with Andre, the method whereby Lucier fashions his compositions is one of presentation rather than transformation. Typically, in each of his works, some acoustic phenomenon is encountered, isolated and projected to the audience. All the activities of the composer are directed toward the magnification of the isolated phenomenon making it clearly perceptible to all listening. From such early works as *Music for Solo Performer* (1965) through the more recent *Shapes of the Sounds from the Board* (1979-80), this procedure has remained essentially unchanged. In the former the composer focuses upon alpha waves and enables the perceiver to experience them in a variety of visual and sonic guises, while in the latter he makes the listener aware of the spatial characteristics inherent in every sonic emanation.

Nowhere, however, is this unique approach to composition more apparent than in *Music for Pure Waves, Bass Drums and Acoustic Pendulums* (1980). To date, this is only one of two works by Lucier which may be considered "percussion pieces" (the other being *Music for Solo Performer*) though it must be said that this very notion of categorization by ensemble is one of the conceits of traditional composition and performance practice which his music has always defied. The score of *Pendulums* is reprinted on the next four pages in its entirety. In addition, the composer has provided the following concise description:

> As the pure sounds flow through the drumheads, causing them to vibrate, the balls bounce against the heads in ever-changing rhythmic patterns, determined by the pitches and volumes of the waves and the resonant characteristics of the drums. As the waves pass through the drums' resonant regions, the heads vibrate more violently, causing the balls to bounce farther away. Sometimes up to a length of two feet. If at the moment a ball returns to a drumhead, the head itself is on an outward phase of its vibratory cycle, the ball is again bounced outward and the size of the pendular swing is maintained or even increased. If, however, the ball meets the head on an inward

95

MUSIC FOR PURE WAVES, BASS DRUMS
AND ACOUSTIC PENDULUMS
for one player with electronics and percussion

Introduction

Electronically-generated sound waves excite the heads of large bass drums, setting into motion ultra-light pendulums which are suspended in front of the drums. The rhythms created as the tips of the pendulums strike the heads of the drums are determined by the pitch and loudness of the waves, the lengths of the pendulums and the resonant characteristics of the drums themselves.

Equipment

4	large bass drums, all the same size
4	matched loudspeakers, small enough for each to stand unseen behind a drum
1	sine wave oscillator
1	quadraphonic amplifier or equivalent amplifiers with 4 loudspeaker terminals
4	ping-pong balls
1	spool of 2 or 4 lb. test monofilament fishing line
2	8-foot tables, if necessary
1	small table

Set-up

Place the drums side by side, their heads facing the audience. Elevate them on tables, if necessary, for unobstructed viewing.

Make 4 acoustic pendulums by gluing a long length of monofilament line to each ping-pong ball. Hang each ball from the ceiling in front of a drum. Raise the rim of each drum by inserting books, paper, foam or other non-resonant material between it and the table top, so that the balls rest firmly against the drumheads. Center each ball exactly in the middle of its drumhead.

Position a loudspeaker directly behind each drum. Set the oscillator and amplifiers on the small table in the middle of the room. Wire the amplifiers to the loudspeakers. Plug the oscillator into the amplifiers, routing its signal equally to all 4 loudspeakers. See Figure 1.

Switch the oscillator frequency range to F x 1, or equivalent. Find and preset the lowest frequency to which the loudspeakers respond. Lower all volume levels to Zero.

Performance

Sit at the electronics table, facing the array of drums. Slowly raise volume levels to a point at which one or more pendulums start oscillating. Throughout the performance manually rotate the frequency tuning dial of the oscillator in one upward sweep, causing sine waves at all frequencies within that sweep to flow through the loudspeakers, exciting the drumheads accordingly. As the heads vibrate more or less actively in response to various frequencies the pendulums are driven away from the heads at various distances, creating continually-changing rhythmic patterns.

Sweep with microscopic slowness so as not to miss any possible pattern and with *continuous motion* so as to make an accurate mapping in time of all resonant, sympathetic, pendular, sonic, and visible phenomena.

Keep volume levels as low as possible, while still maintaining effective pendular motion.

A performance is over when a frequency region is reached in which the drums no longer respond. As that situation becomes clear, lower all volume levels to Zero. An average performance time is about 15 minutes. See Figure 2.

Installation Version

Set up from 1 to 4 drums, pendulums, and loudspeakers in the manner described above. Position the oscillator and amplifiers, however, out of view of visitors.

Tune the oscillator to a resonant frequency common to all the drums. Then for the duration of the installation let changes in temperature, humidity, and other environmental conditions alter the tensions of the drumheads, thereby varying the pendular motion and its resulting sonic and rhythmic manifestations.

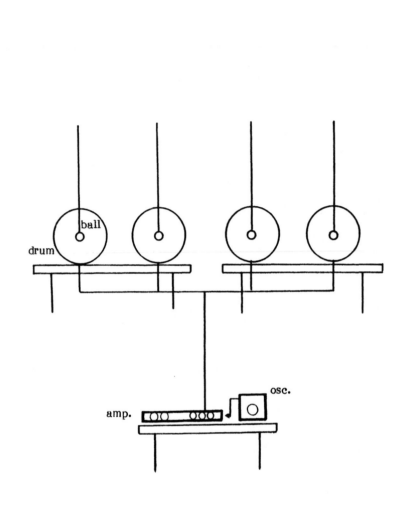

FIGURE 1

SINE SWEEP

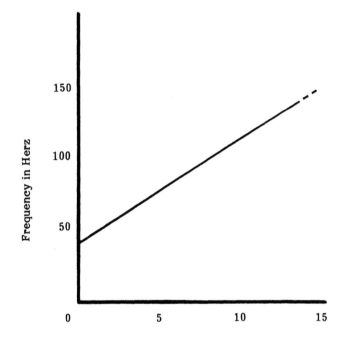

time in minutes

FIGURE 2

or negative phase, the motion is dampened and
the ball may be stopped dead.[7]

Lucier proposes two different modes of presentation; one for traditional concert performance and the other as an installation in a museum or gallery space. The concert version involves all four bass drums. Over a period of approximately fifteen minutes, one sine tone rises very slowly creating the sonic experience described above. The installation is, of necessity, somewhat more static. One to four bass drums may be used and the oscillator is tuned to one pitch common to all their resonant frequencies. In this case variation in the sonic result arises not from changes in the frequency of the pure tone but from random fluctuations in environmental conditions (temperature, humidity, etc.) which alter the tensions of the drumheads and eventually the speed of the pendular motion.

Central to any understanding of this work is the recognition that its form is identified exclusively with the isolation and magnification of one particular acoustic phenomenon. The unique configuration of *Pendulums* is derived from the internal structure of the sine tone. The composer has created a situation in which this simple sound is articulated in several different ways: one sonic (tapping on the drum), the other visual (the swing of the pendulum). Everything that affects these two interconnected motions is determined by the basic properties of the acoustic matter employed. The pure wave (its frequency and volume), the drum (its resonance regions and skin tension), and the room (its temperature and humidity) all affect the sonic/visual results. At no time, however, are these parameters subject to manipulation by the composer. Instead, he accepts the random and spontaneous sonic/visual display which their fortuitous interactions produce.

The idea of rendering sound "visible" is not one that is new to Lucier's work. In several pieces which precede *Pendulums* - *The Queen of the South* (1972), *Tyndall Orchestrations* (1977), *Ghosts* (1978), *Directions of Sounds from the Bridge* (1978) - he had already addressed this issue. In the first two, sound waves cause momentary, visible alterations in the shape of the various physical materials toward which they are directed. In

Ghosts "one performer carrying a sound sensitive light, searches through a pure sound wave environment for bumps of sound, caused by imperfections (reflections, absorptions, etc.) in the environment, which cause the light to turn on."[8] This procedure of using sound waves to trigger lighting devices is also employed - though in somewhat different ways - in *Directions* and where the directional characteristics of sonic phenomena are delineated for the eye as well as the ear.

In *Pendulums*, however, sound is made visible in a manner quite different from each of the above. The invisible waves of air pressure produced by the sine tone are "translated" into the visible movement of the ball. As the pendulum swings back and forth, it traces the vibrations emanating from the loudspeaker. Its regular rocking motion creates a perfect visual correlate to the cyclic structure of the pure wave.

It is important to note that transference from the sonic to the visual medium is not accomplished through a direct translation of the sine wave to the pendulum but rather through an intermediary - the bass drum. This, in turn, effects another kind of synesthesia as the sound of the original pure tone is also "translated" into the tapping produced when the ball hits the drum. Changes in the frequency of the pure tone produce changes in both the speed and volume of the tapping sound. Thus, the original sound wave is rendered in two different ways - one sonic, the other visual.

In this composition the composer reveals hidden dimensions of the apparently simple acoustical phenomenon known as the sine tone and documents the complexity of its inner structure. Moreover, he reveals an inner structure which is remarkably at odds with all outward appearances. The pure tone which activates the pendulums is, in reality, a series of cyclic repetitions of pressure waves in the air which the ear synthesizes into a single sustained sound. When, however, it is translated into the movement and sound of a ball striking a drum, it is re-created in a sonic/visual guise which is discrete and repetitive and clearly suggestive of the tone's inner vibratory cycle. Thus, what is exposed is the discontinuous nature of a phenomenon which, when experienced under ordinary listening conditions, appears quite steady and continuous. That which on the surface appears to be a single uninflected gesture becomes - when magnified - a rich, volatile sonic event constantly varying in form.

Significantly, not only is the sine tone articulated in this manner but also the sonic characteristics of the drums themselves are brought into the audible/visible framework of the composition. In the concert version of the work, this is particularly apparent. As the pure wave slowly rises it passes through the various resonant regions of the drums. Each time this happens, there is a rather dramatic change in the motion of the pendulums. Since, in this version, all four drums are to be used, no two of which will be identical with respect to their constituent resonant characteristics, the sonic result will consist of four distinct, though variable, rhythmic patterns. In general, then, irregularities among the four pendular motions will be the direct result of differences among the four drums.

In addition, the composer creates a visual and sonic enlargement of the sound system itself. The oscillator produces sound by exciting vibrations in the speaker cone. These are translated into the larger vibrations of the drum skin; which are, in turn, translated into the most visible and, in a sense, most audible manifestations of the original vibrations - those of the bouncing ball striking the drumhead. When, as the composer pointed out earlier:

> ...a ball returns to a drumhead when the head
> itself is on an outward phase of its vibratory
> cycle, the ball is again bounced outward and the
> size of the pendular swing is maintained or even
> increased. If, however, the ball meets the head
> on an inward or negative phase, the motion is
> dampened and the ball may be stopped dead.[9]

The rather dramatic fluctuations and frequent irregularities in the movement of the ball could not be caused by the steady, unvarying vibrations of the sine wave. Rather, they result from the interplay between the drum and the pendulum, both of which are excited in different ways by the pure tone. Thus, the pendulum and its constituent tapping sounds are not only manifestations of the pure tone's internal vibrations but

102

are also visual and aural translations of the mechanism by which those vibrations are transformed into an audible acoustic event.

In summary, the composer focuses upon three specific phenomena within his structure – three aspects of the acoustic manifestation of the pure tone: the sine wave itself; the tapping sound (the source of the alternate sonic representation of the sine wave) and its visual correlate, the swing of the pendulum (the source of the visual representation of the sine wave); and, the sound system itself (the mechanism by which these phenomena become manifest to the perceiver). All three are isolated and magnified. The oscillator, drum and ball produce the alternate sonic/visual representation of the pure tone while the sound system allows one type of sound to be translated into another. The structure of this piece, then, is a process which reveals not only the nature of its source materials but also the very means by which those materials are perceived.

Clearly, in this work, the composer is concerned with neither the creation of some new sound structure nor the transformation of sonic matter. Rather, his goal is to project sound in such a way that the listener becomes intensely aware of the nature of the phenomenon he is perceiving. In this music, sound exists not as the means to some "formal" or "expressive" ends but rather, as an end in itself. It is an art of pure presence, devoid of all vestige of personal metaphor; an art in which sound is the object of perception but never the subject of discourse. As such, the perceiver is forced to re-evaluate his own position vis-a-vis the artwork. Through the dual synesthesia identified above, the sonic object is magnified until the listener is made conscious of its presence to him and, simultaneously, his own presence to it. The experience is circular. As the listener becomes conscious of the object of his perceptions, he also becomes aware of the act of perceiving and, finally, of himself as the perceiving being. Perception, then, becomes the ground for cognition and the source for all consciousness of presence, both of the object and the perceiver. Thus, while experiencing the work, the listener becomes aware of himself making that transcendent leap from perception to cognition – an awareness of presence. In this sense Lucier's art may be seen as the culmination of a post-Cartesian dialectic in which perception is understood, not as the product of the thinking mind, but as the source of all thought.

As with many of this composer's works, in *Music for Pure Waves, Bass Drums and Acoustic Pendulums* the medium becomes the ground for experience. Materials are never used to fabricate dramatic scenarios nor to express abstract relations. Instead, they are made present to the listener in some heightened way. In Lucier's work the process of composition becomes a process of "presencing" through which the listener himself rises to the forefront of the aesthetic experience. His is an art which seeks not to share a personal vision but, instead, leads the perceiver to recognize that the only basis for a communality of experience lies in the sheer individuality of each perception.

What is revealed through this music is the fact that an art's most vital function is to re-create the condition of being - not the experiences of one's life but that perpetual state of transcendence which is the very substance of life. As the poet Cid Corman notes: "Art has no object but is an object through which realization occurs..."[10] The triumph of a work such as *Pendulums* lies in the simple yet elegant way it leads each listener to an awareness of those variable conditions of perception which enable him to appropriate the phenomena of the world as meaningful for himself.

...no ideas but in things.[11]

1. William Carlos Williams, *Paterson* (New York: New Directions Paperbooks, 1963), p. ii.

2. Lawrence Weschler, *Seeing is Forgetting the Name of the Thing One Sees* (Berkeley, California: University of California Press, 1982), p. 200.

3. *Ibid.*, p. 127.

4. Gregoire Muller, *The New Avant-Garde* (New York: Praeger Publishers, 1972), p. 13.

5. Alvin Lucier, "The Tools of My Trade", *Sonus* (Vol. 2, No. 1), p. 13.

6. *Ibid.*, p. 15.

7. *Ibid.*, p. 18.

8. *Ibid.*, p. 18.

9. *Ibid.*, p. 18.

10. Cid Corman, "Staying With It" from *The Act of Poetry and Two Other Essays* (Santa Barbara, California: Black Sparrow Press, 1976), p. 3.

11. Williams, *op. cit.* p. 11.

Index

Thomas DeLio (b. 1951, Bronx, New York) is a noted composer and theorist. He studied at The New England Conservatory of Music and Brown University where he received a Ph.D. in an interdisciplinary studies program combining mathematics, music and the visual arts. His articles on the music of Luigi Dallapiccola, Elliott Carter, Iannis Xenakis, John Cage, Philip Glass and Robert Ashley have appeared in *The Musical Quarterly*, *Perspectives of New Music*, *The Journal of Music Theory*, *Artforum* and *Interface*. In addition, he is co-founder and co-editor of *Sonus*, an interdisciplinary journal devoted to the most progressive ideas in the arts today. As a composer he has distinguished himself in the area of computer aided composition and as the creator of a series of live electronic sound installations. His music is published by Dorn Publications and recorded on the Spectrum label. He has taught at Clark University and The New England Conservatory of music and is currently a member of the faculty of the Department of Music at the University of Maryland at College Park.